TACTICAL DRUMMING
GROOVE SURVIVAL GUIDE

BY JOHN OWENS, PH.D.
ARMY BAND VETERAN DRUMMER

Tactical Drumming: Groove Survival Guide

www.tacticaldrumming.com

First Printing, 2023

ISBN: 978-1-954270-25-1
eBook ISBN: 978-1-954270-25-8

Imprint: Independently Published

TABLE OF CONTENTS

WHAT IS TACTICAL DRUMMING?

Tactical drumming is a focused approach to learning drums that zeros in on the essential grooves you need to know. Most importantly, it eliminates drum set rhythms that are rarely used and prioritizes beats that are played all the time. This approach is similar to military basic training, where soldiers concentrate on the skills they need to be proficient, strong, and successful in a variety of combat situations. Likewise, this approach centers on rhythms that will make you a solid, skillful, and well-trained drummer. By learning the grooves in this book, you will be prepared to play in just about every style.

TACTICAL DRUMMING STRATEGY: DRUM SET

- Learn the core groove in each style.
- Eliminate unneeded beats.
- Master groove variations that can fit in multiple musical genres.
- Enhance playing and style with pro tips.
- Concisely study the background and nuance of each groove.
- Listen to real world examples of each groove through classic tunes.

In this guide, each section includes the core groove, how to play it, suggested listening in various styles, and effective variations that will give you the skills you need to play grooves in just about every musical situation.

Why create an approach that focuses only on vital drum grooves? In my experiences as a drummer for the US Army Band, Disneyland, playing thousands of jazz, rock, pop, and country gigs, touring with various bands, and teaching beginning to advanced drummers for many years, I have found that there are really only a handful of grooves that are used all the time. Are there some specialty beats that are specific to obscure styles? Of course there are, but in the end, there are just a handful of grooves that are used all the time. That is what this book is about, teaching you the grooves you need to survive and thrive.

ELEVATE YOUR DRUMMING AT:

www.tacticaldrumming.com

HOW TO USE THIS BOOK

Each groove in this book is strategically broken down to learn with ease. Tactical drumming can be used in order, as the most popular and easiest grooves are at the beginning. Or, you can start with the grooves you like and listen to the most, as this is a good way dig into beats that are useful and enjoyable to you.

Here is a list of what is included in each section and how to approach each groove.

- **THE GROOVE:** This is fundamental groove (always start here).
- **ABOUT IT:** Some basic information about the groove, which includes details about the rhythms origins, use, and tips.
- **LEARN IT:** Step by step instructions on how to learn each part of the fundamental groove and put it together.
- **PRO TIP:** Sage advice on how to elevate the groove and make you sound awesome on the drums.
- **LISTEN TO IT:** List of sample tunes that use the groove. I highly recommend finding and listening to these recordings, as this will help you master the rhythm and feel.
- **WATCH IT:** Link to an instructional video that shows you how to systematically play the groove.
- **RHYTHMIC VARIATIONS:** Three practical variations for each groove, which can be used in a variety of musical settings.
- **ELEVATING THE GROOVE:** A couple of alternative ways to play the groove that make it more intricate and nuanced.

TACTICAL DRUMMING

DRUM SET BASICS

THE DRUM SET

To play the grooves in this book, all you need is a basic drum kit/drum set, which includes the following:

- Snare Drum
- Bass Drum
- Hi-Hat
- Ride Cymbal
- Tom (High)
- Tom (Low)

If you are right handed, below is the most common set up. If you are left-handed (lefty or southpaw), you can just flip the kit around or play "open face," which is simply putting the ride cymbal on your left (this is a very common technique used by left handed players).

RIGHT HANDED DRUM SET

Photo by Milton Owens (2023): Used with permission.

OPEN FACE (LEFTY/SOUTHPAW DRUM SET)

Below is an example of "open face" drumming. Note: The ride cymbal is on the left side of the kit, which allows a left-handed drummer to play the ride cymbal with the left hand with ease. In a survey of left-handed drummers I conducted in 2023, I found that most southpaw drummers play open face. However, a number of lefty drummers "flip" the drum set, which means they play a mirror image of the left handed kit; so, the hi-hat and snare would be on the left hand side of the kit (not pictured). In the end, it is really up to the drummer how they want to set it up.

Photo by Milton Owens (2023): Used with permission.

STICKING

The sticking provided for each groove will make it easier to play the rhythms. The symbols used are *R* for right and *L* for left. I suggest using the recommended sticking, even if it seems difficult at first, as it will be beneficial in the long run. If you are a left-handed player (lefty) I suggest using the opposite sticking.

Using *R* for right hand and *L* for left hand, here is an example of the sticking for a paradiddle: RLRR LRLL. Below you can see the paradiddle notated.

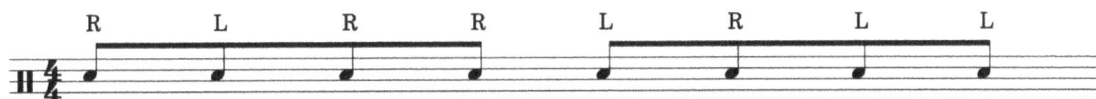

PARTS OF THE DRUM SET

From left to right: Hi-Hat, Crash Cymbal, Snare Drum, High Tom, Bass Drum, Ride Cymbal, Low Tom.

Photo by Milton Owens (2023): Used with permission.

BASS DRUM

Also known as the kick drum. This is the large drum that is played with a foot pedal, which is usually 22 or 20 inches in diameter. This serves as the foundation of each groove. Please note: Bass drums do come in other sizes, such as 18 or 24 inches, but they are always the largest drum in the set.

SNARE DRUM

Drum that is typically 14 inches in diameter, though other sizes are available. This drum will be used to play the backbeat of most grooves. It is called a snare because there are snares (strings, wires, and originally animal guts) across the bottom head that create the poppy "snare" sound.

HI-HAT

Pair of cymbals (usually 14 inches, though other sizes are used) that are controlled by a foot pedal, which are pressed together so they can be played "tightly" together or "loosely" apart. The reason it is a called a hi-hat is because the original design (known as the "lowboy") was on the floor; then, it was raised up and became known as the hi-hat.

RIDE CYMBAL

The large cymbal (typically 20 to 22 inches) on the right in the photo above is the ride cymbal. You can play any of the cymbal rhythms in the book on the ride cymbal, but this will be especially important when playing the swing groove.

TOMS

There are two main toms, which are the high tom and low tom. Of course, many drum sets come with three toms that include an additional high tom or another low tom. Sometimes the low tom is referred to as the floor tom, as traditionally this drum has its own legs and sits on the floor like a table.

DRUM NOTATION QUICK GUIDE

Below is a quick guide of how to read the drum set notation that will be used in this book. Specifically, it shows you what each symbol (musical notation) represents on the musical staff.

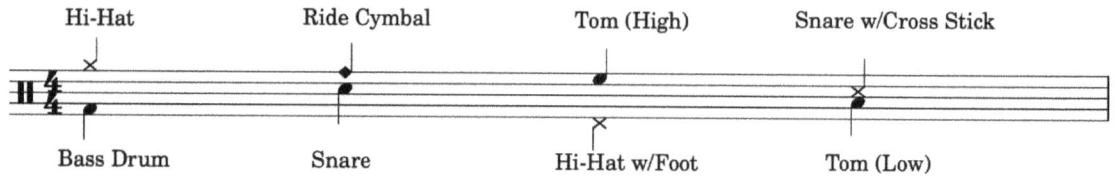

NOTATION COUNTING GUIDE

Quarter Notes: To get started, just count 1, 2, 3, 4 and play on each beat. I suggest alternating your sticking; so, RLRL.

Eighth Notes: Next, play the eighth notes indicated below, which are counted as 1 & 2 & 3 & 4 &. At this point, use the alternating sticking above (RLRLRLRL).

Sixteenth Notes: The sixteenth notes are counted as 1e&a 2e&a 3e&a 4e&a. Keep the same sticking as above (RLRL) and try to play it as evenly as possible.

Notated Groove Example: Since this book is focused on drum set rhythms, here is an example of a simple groove that incorporates all three rhythms above. Please note the repeat markings at the beginning and end of the measure, which mean to play it again.

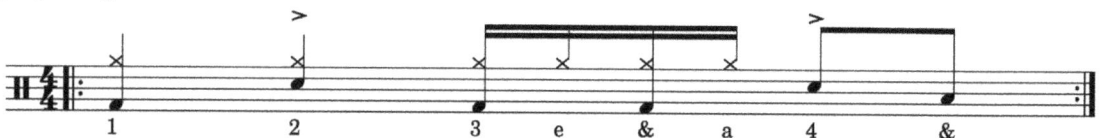

10

TACTICAL HANDS

Playing drum set is really all about your hands and feet. While you can jump right into playing grooves, here is some tactical advise on the skills you will need to play the rhythms in this book. As a drummer, a good approach to training yourself is to practice a few of these exercises each day, which will make you stronger and faster.

HANDS

MIGHTY V

When holding your sticks, the best shape to make is the *Mighty V*. By keeping your hands in this shape, with your palms down, you will have solid technique when you strike any drum and/or cymbal. Basically, you should keep the Mighty V at all times and maintain the integrity of the shape as you move around the kit.

ON SNARE

Take note of the grip and V shape in the center of the drum head.

Photo by Milton Owens (2023): Used with permission.

SNARE & HI-HAT

As you can see, the V shape is maintained in the hands, but they are crossed over.

Photo by Milton Owens (2023): Used with permission.

SNARE & RIDE

Likewise, the Mighty V is maintained as you move to the ride cymbal.

Photo by Milton Owens (2023): Used with permission.

SNARE & TOM HAND POSITION

Here you can observe the same *Mighty V* shape when moving to the toms. To play with accuracy and speed, it is essential to maintain this technique.

Photo by Milton Owens (2023): Used with permission.

TACTICAL DRUMMING

GRIP

No matter when drum or cymbal you are playing, your grip stays the same. To get the best grip just grab your sticks between your thumb and pointer finger. Now, gently wrap the rest of you fingers around the stick. Be sure to keep your palm down you are all set.

MATCHED GRIP (TOP VIEW)

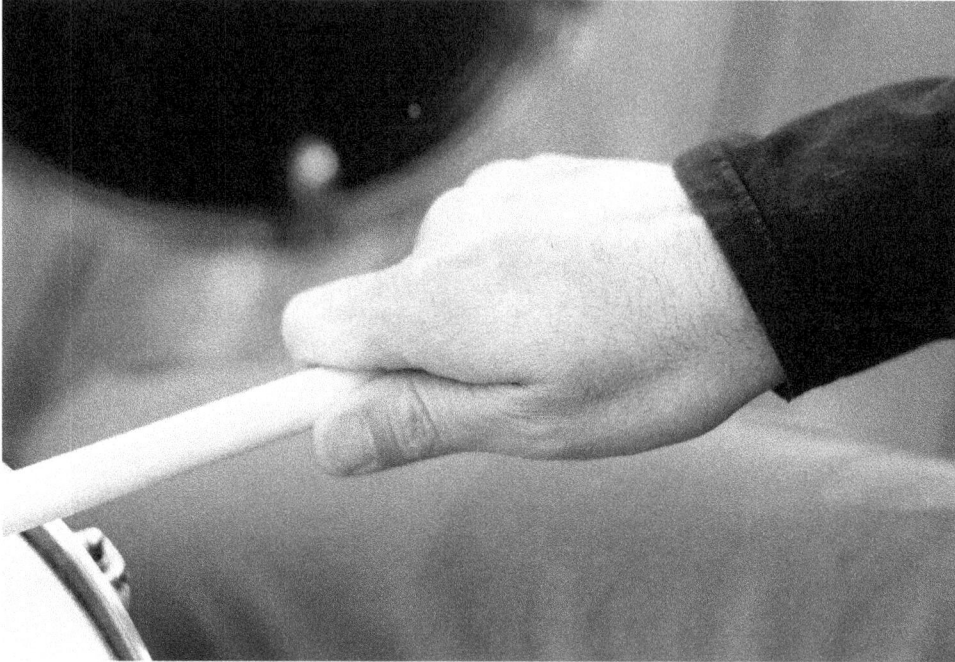

Photo by Milton Owens (2023): Used with permission.

MATCHED GRIP (BOTTOM VIEW)

Photo by Milton Owens (2023): Used with permission.

TRADITIONAL GRIP

One other approach to playing drums is traditional grip. Many drummers still play this grip because it is a tradition that was used by military drummers in the 1700 and 1800s. In addition, many influential jazz drummers in the early 1900s, such as Buddy Rich, Art Blakey, Chic Webb, and Gene Krupa, all played with traditional grip. This grip is still used today on drum set and marching percussion.

Here is a quick explanation of how play traditional grip.
- Put your left hand out like you are going to shake someone's hand.
- Cradle the stick between your thumb and pointer finger.
- Place the stick on the end of your middle finger (like a shelf)
- Connect your thumb and pointer finger.
- Keep the top of your thumb parallel to the ground (this is starting position).
- Now, rotate your wrist to the left, with the palm of your hand to the sky.
- To make a stroke, rotate your wrist back to the starting position as you hit the drumhead.
- Please note: The right hand used matched grip, as only left is played traditionally.

TRADITIONAL GRIP EXAMPLE

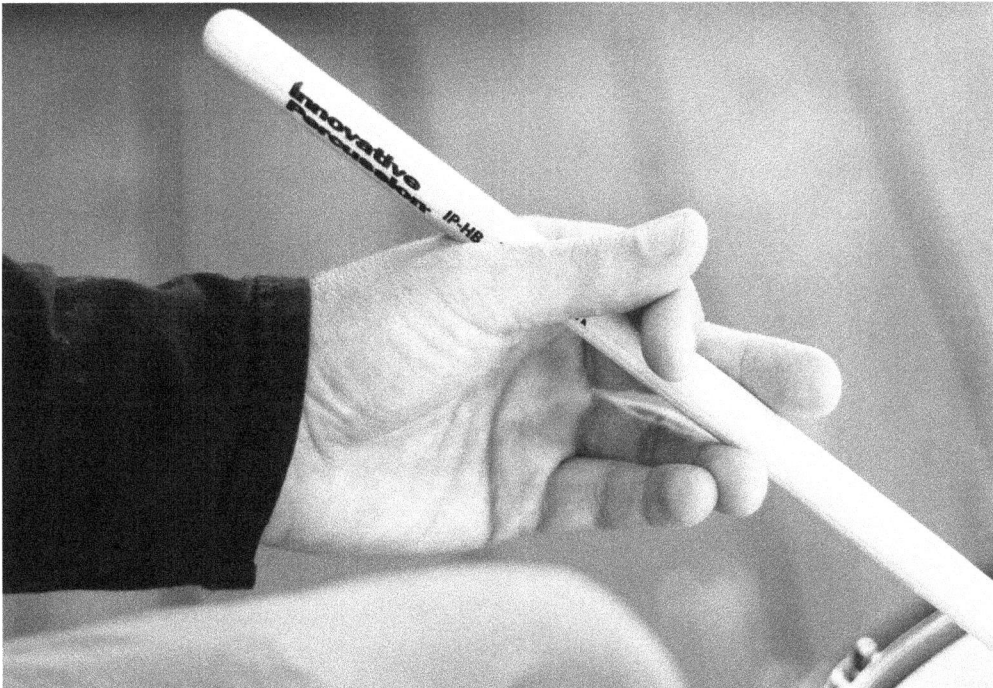

Photo by Milton Owens (2023): Used with permission.

WATCH IT

Here is a quick video on how to play traditional grip:
https://www.youtube.com/watch?v=zeJRf4xvwx0

FEELING TIME

Below are a series of sticking exercises to help you feel time, develop your singles, doubles, and triples, and start building your chops (power and speed).

R R R R L L L L

EIGHTS
Eights (Hand to Hand)

R R R R R R R R L L L L L L L L

SINGLES
Singles (RLRL)

R R R R R R R R R L R L R L R L R L R L R L
L L L L L L L L L R L R L R L R L R L R L R

DOUBLES
Doubles (RR LL): First measure is a check pattern.

R L R L R L R L R R L L R R L L R R L L R R L L

THREES
Threes (RRR LLL)

R R R R R R R R R R R R R R R R R R R R R R R R
L L L L L L L L L L L L L L L L L L L L L L L L

ACCENTS
Accents (Bucks)

R R R R R R R R R R R R R R R R
L L L L L L L L L L L L L L L L

TACTICAL FEET

To play drum set well and master the essential grooves listed in this book, you will need to be able to play a number of patterns with your feet. While this section does not include all of the bass and hi-hat patterns in the book, it does provide the most common patters and elements you will need to play each beat.

HI-HAT VS BASS DRUM

I recommend the *heal up* approach, which means that you play on the bass and/or hi-hat pedal with your heal up. This is done by pushing down on the pedal with the ball of your foot. You can see this demonstrated in the image below.

HEAL TOE TECHNIQUE

Photo by Milton Owens (2023): Used with permission.

SINGLES

Singles (Quarters and eights: BD & HH)

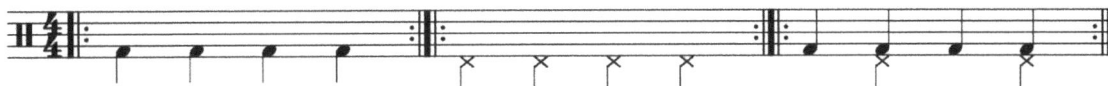

TWO BEAT
Independence (three variations)

DOUBLE EIGHTHS
Doubles (double patterns: BD only)

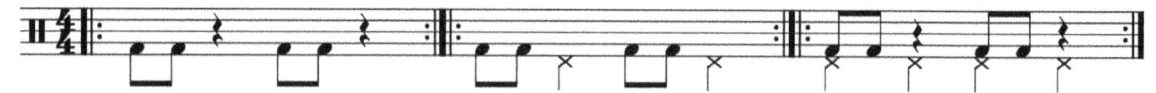

BOSSA BASS PATTERN
Independence (three variations)

SAMBA BASS PATTERN
Independence (three variations)

TOP POPULAR GROOVES

POP/ROCK

THE GROOVE

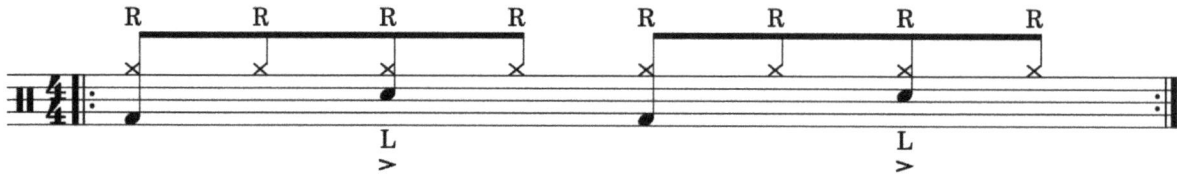

ABOUT IT

With origins in Rhythm & Blues from mid-1950s, the Pop/Rock groove can be heard driving millions of tunes. It is used in rock, pop, country, and other genres. It is also the first rhythm that I teach my students because it is easy to learn and allows them to play along with tons of music.

LISTEN TO IT

- *Thunderstruck* by AC/DC
- *Billie Jean* by Michael Jackson
- *I Gotta Feeling* by Black Eyed Peas

LEARN IT: BREAKDOWN

STEP 1: ONE HAND
Start by playing the hi-hat only with your dominant hand. This is played with the right hand, but it can also be played with the left (if you are a lefty).

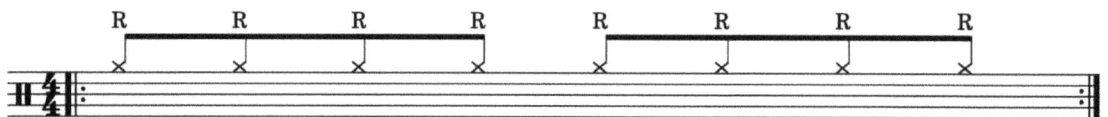

STEP 2: TWO HANDS
Then, add two and four on the snare. A good way to think about this is right, right, together.

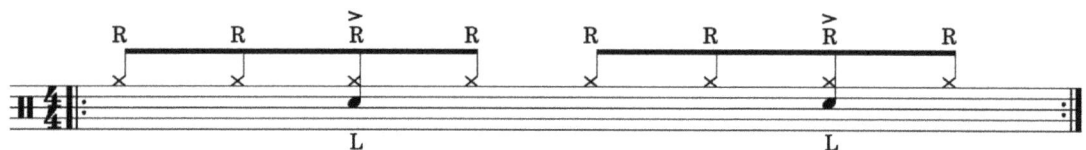

20

STEP 3: BASS & CYMBAL

Stop playing the snare part (left hand), but keep the hi-hat (right hand) going. Now, add the bass drum (on beats 1 & 3) using your foot.

STEP 4: ALL TOGETHER

Slowly play all three parts together. Once you are comfortable with the groove, you can increase the tempo. Be sure to accent 2 & 4 on the snare drum.

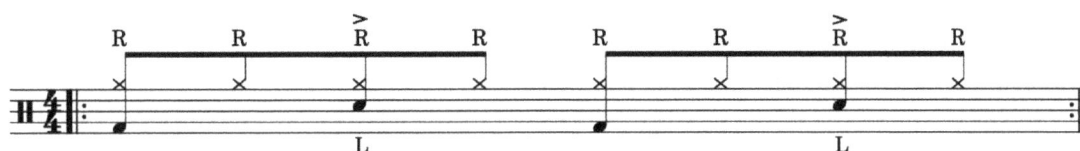

PRO TIP

Make the bass and snare parts stand out by keeping the hi-hat lower in volume and accenting the bass and snare. The snare drum should especially stand out, as this is essence of the groove. I suggest really laying into the snare (hit it hard and in the center), as this is the part that makes your listeners move to the music.

WATCH IT

Find my Pop/Rock video demo at:
https://www.youtube.com/watch?v=Ech9ZSdVPWU

POP/ROCK: RHYTHMIC VARIATIONS

COMMON ROCK VARIATION

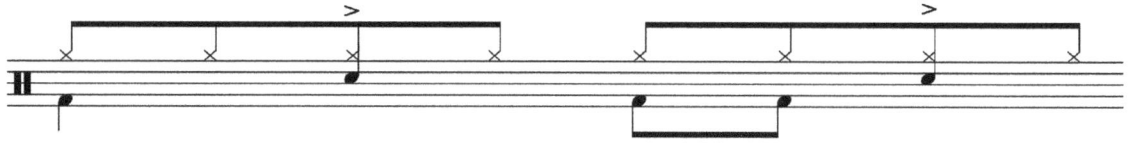

"WE WILL ROCK YOU"

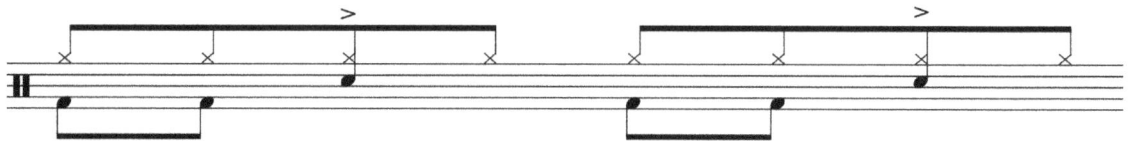

SYNCOPATED ROCK/POP

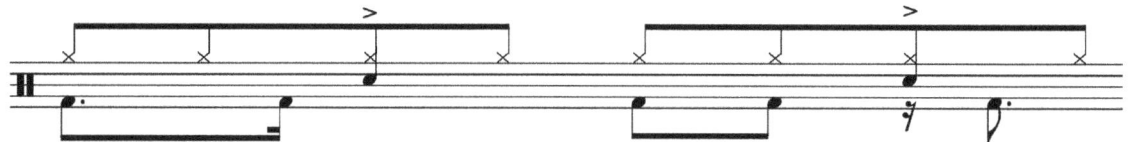

ELEVATING THE GROOVE

COMMON ROCK W/LEFT FOOT HI-HAT

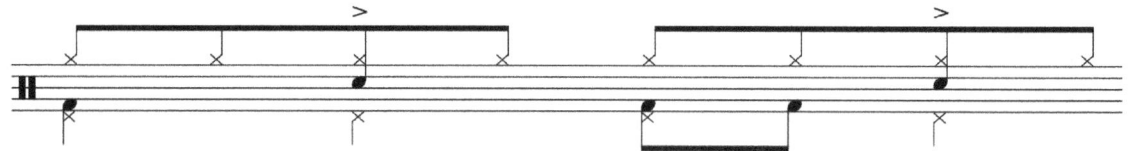

UP BEAT 8THS W/LEFT FOOT HI-HAT

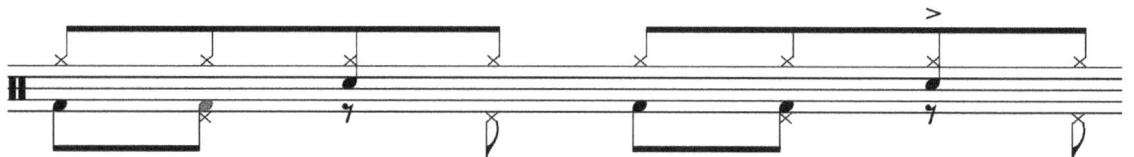

LATIN POP

THE GROOVE

ABOUT IT

Latin Pop is the fusion of grooves from the Caribbean, Central America, and South America with mainstream popular music. This groove is syncopated (rhythm that occurs off the beat) and makes people want to dance. Some pioneer artists in this genre include Gloria Estefan (1980s), Ricky Martin (1990s), and Jennifer Lopez (2000s). The beats in this style are played by a drummer, Latin percussionists (conga, shakers, etc.), or programmed into a drum machine. The essence of this rhythm is the offbeat snare drum, which gives it a "Latin" vibe.

LISTEN TO IT

- *Despacito by* Luis Fonsi
- *Hips Don't Lie* by Shakira
- *La Cancion* by Bad Bunny

LEARN IT: BREAKDOWN

STEP 1: ONE HAND
Start by playing the hi-hat alone (this is just quarter notes). While doing this, listen to one of examples below to get the feel.

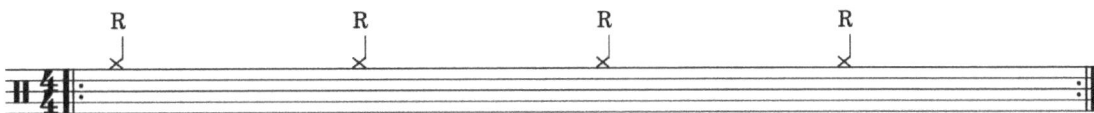

STEP 2: TWO HANDS
Next, slowly play the hi-hat and snare parts together. It is important to use the sticking indicated, as this will make it easier to apply to the drum set.

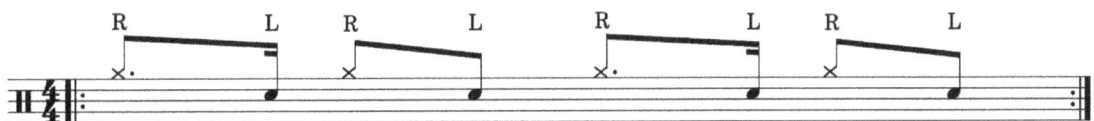

STEP 3: BASS & CYMBAL

Stop playing the snare part (left hand), but keep the hi-hat (right hand) going. Now, add the bass drum using your foot.

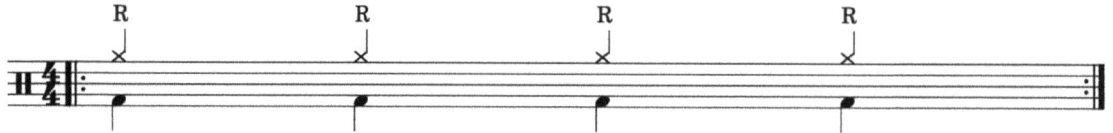

STEP 4: ALL TOGETHER

Once you have locked in the hi-hat/snare drum rhythms, put together all three parts. Do this slowly at first; then, speed it up.

PRO TIP

Emphasize the snare drum part (left hand) and relax when playing. This groove feels best when it lays back, which means to play the snare drum part a little behind the beat.

WATCH IT

Find my Latin Pop video demo at:

www.youtube.com/watch?v=X3H7Yhzv_5w&t=5s

LATIN POP: RHYTHMIC VARIATIONS

EIGHTH NOTE HI-HAT VARIATION

EXTRA SNARE

SYNCOPATED SNARE

ELEVATING THE GROOVE

LIFTED HI-HAT W/THREES

OFFBEAT HI-HAT

DANCE

THE GROOVE

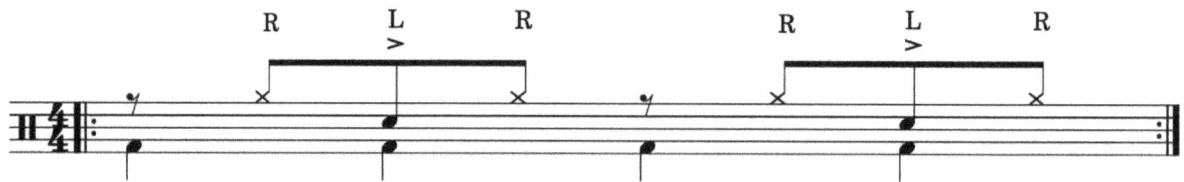

ABOUT IT

Used in dance music for over fifty years, the Dance Groove is the lifeblood of disco, EDM (Electronic Dance Music), and popular dance music today. This includes music from artists like Chic (1970s), Madonna (1980s), Daft Punk (1990s), Lady Gaga (2000s), Katy Perry (2010s), and Billie Eilish (2020s). The core of this groove is the offbeat hi-hat and pounding bass drum that makes people want to get up and dance.

LISTEN TO IT

- *Poker Face* by Lady Gaga
- *YMCA* by The Village People
- *Firework* by Katy Perry

LEARN IT: BREAKDOWN

STEP 1: ONE HAND

Play the *backbeat* (2 & 4) on the snare drum with your left hand. This can also be played with the right, if you are a lefty.

STEP 2: TWO HANDS

Play just the hands, which is the hi-hat and snare drum rhythms. Pay special attention to the sticking. Also, be sure to accent the snare drum part.

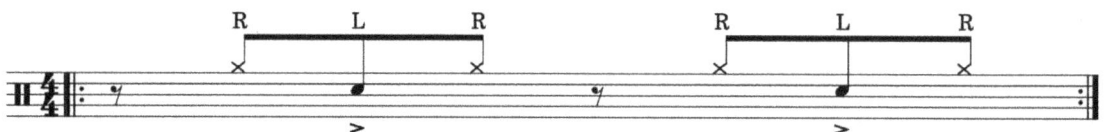

STEP 3: BASS & CYMBAL

On each beat, play quarter notes on the bass drum. Then, add the backbeat (2 & 4) on the snare drum.

STEP 4: ALL TOGETHER

Once you have mastered the hands (hi-hat/snare rhythms), play the hi-hat/snare drum parts while maintaining the bass drum. Be sure to keep accenting 2 & 4 on the snare drum.

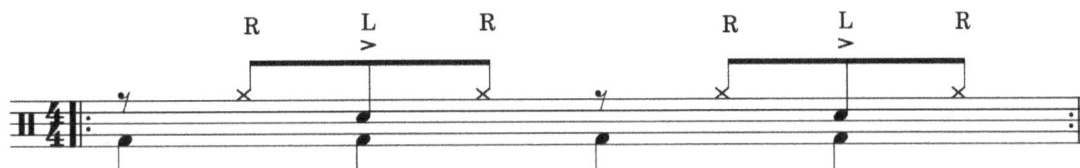

PRO TIP

You can play the cymbal three different ways: (1) Tight closed hi-hat; (2) open hi-hat; (3) ride cymbal (I like it on the bell). When playing the open hi-hat, be sure to keep the sound open (loose hi-hat), but short. Use the video below to hear the groove and open hi-hat technique that fits the style.

WATCH IT

Find my Dance Groove video at:
https://www.youtube.com/watch?v=gnMYL49PqdQ

DANCE: RHYTHMIC VARIATIONS

LITTLE EXTRA

16ᵀᴴ VARIATION – NO HI-HAT LIFT

LINEAR SYNCOPATION

ELEVATING THE GROOVE

16ᵀᴴ NOTE VARIATION WITH HI-HAT LIST

LIFTED HI-HAT W/THREES

HIP-HOP/FUNK

THE GROOVE

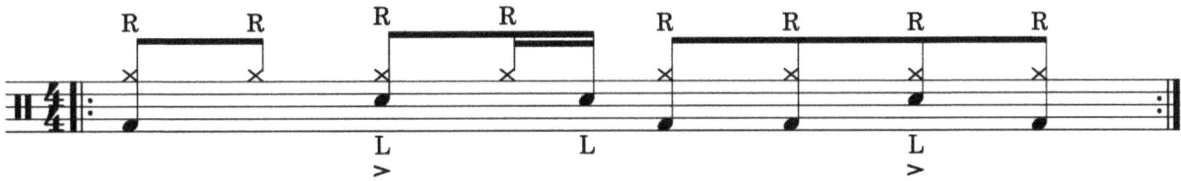

ABOUT IT

Since hip-hop grooves are derived from funk, the essence of this rhythm is to make it syncopated and funky. Funk grooves were pioneered by drummers like Clyde Stubblefield (drummer for James Brown) and are still sampled by modern rap artists, which serve as the foundation of their music. There are a ton of hip-hop/funk grooves, but this is one of the most common rhythms in the style. Plus, it is a blast to play and can be used with a number of hip-hop or funk tunes.

LISTEN TO IT

- *Impeach the President* by The Honey Drippers
- *X Goin Give it to Ya* by DMX (Explicit, but a clean version is available)
- *Barbie Dreams* by Nikki Minaj (Explicit, but a clean version is available)

LEARN IT: BREAKDOWN

STEP 1: ONE HAND
Play just the cymbal part with your dominant hand. This is played with the right hand, but it can also be played with the left (if you are a southpaw drummer).

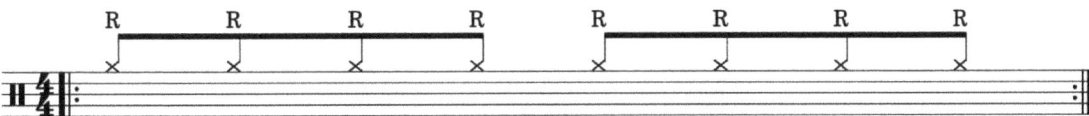

STEP 2: TWO HANDS
From there, play the hi-hat and snare part, this will require some coordination. Be sure to stress the accented notes on the snare.

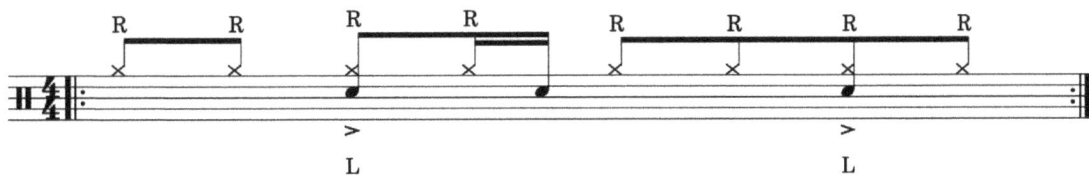

STEP 3: BASS & CYMBAL

Stop playing the snare part (left hand), but keep the hi-hat (right hand) going. Now, add the bass drum using your foot.

STEP 4: ALL TOGETHER

Slowly play all three parts together. Once you are comfortable with the groove, you can increase the tempo. Be sure to accent 2 & 4 on the snare drum. Remember, to emphasize the bass and snare parts to make this groove funky and hip.

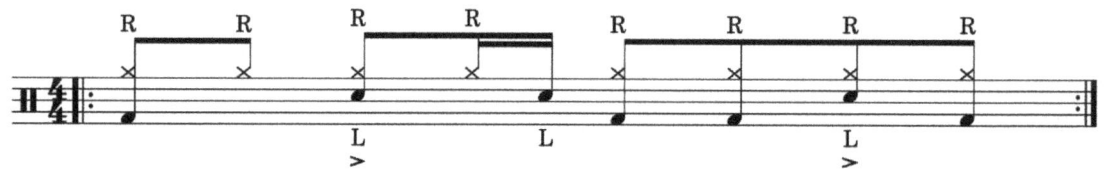

PRO TIP

To really make this groove have character, be sure to keep the non-accented snare notes really low. These are called taps or ghost notes, which subtly add to the feel of the rhythm.

WATCH IT

Find my Hip-Hop/Funk video at:

https://www.youtube.com/watch?v=M4_07jZa6Qk

HIP-HOP/FUNK: RHYTHMIC VARIATIONS

FUNKY DRUMMER

FAB FREDDY GROOVE

PARADIDDLE FUNK

ELEVATING THE GROOVE

OLD SCHOOL HIP-HOP WITH OFF BEAT HI-HAT

FUNKY ENOUGH WITH OFF BEAT HI-HAT

COUNTRY

THE GROOVE

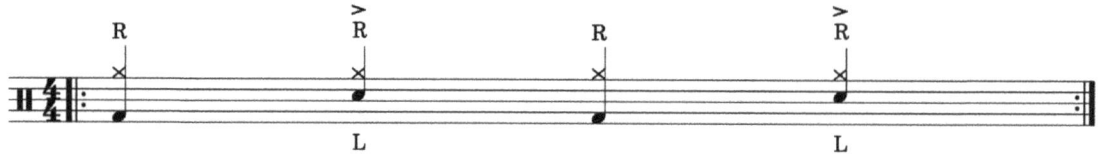

ABOUT IT

Initially, country music did not include drums. However, the country music groove mimicked the rhythm played by the bass, guitar, and mandolin, which were used in bluegrass and early country western music. Overtime, drums were added to this style. While drums were not permitted in the Grand Ole Opry (Home of Country Music) until the mid-1940s, by the 1950s drums and percussion were core part of the music. Eventually, country drumming became more prevalent to include its own unique styles, such as the train beat used by W.S. Holland, the drummer for Johnny Cash. The key to this style of drumming is emphasizing the bass and snare, which mirror the bass fiddle (downbeats) and guitar (upbeats).

LISTEN TO IT

- *Follow Your Arrow* by Kacey Musgraves
- *Folsom Prison Blues* by Johnny Cash
- *Redneck Women* by Gretchen Wilson

LEARN IT: BREAKDOWN

STEP 1: ONE HAND

Play quarter notes with the right hand (left if you are a lefty) on the hi-hat or ride cymbal.

STEP 2: TWO HANDS

Add 2 and 4 on the snare drum while keeping the hi-hat quarter notes going.

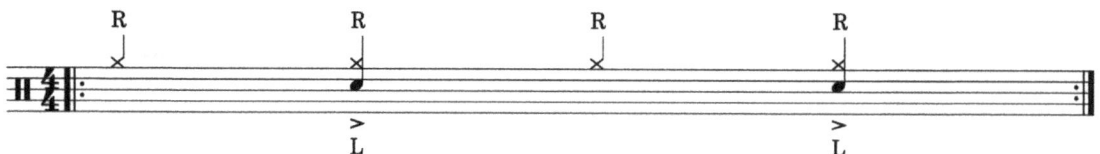

STEP 3: BASS & CYMBAL

Continue playing the hi-hat quarter notes and add the bass drum on 1 & 3.

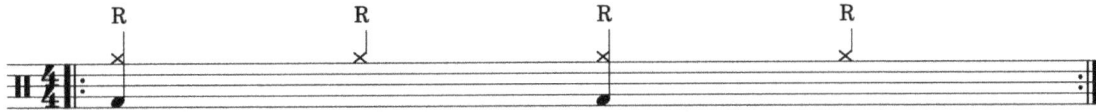

STEP 4: ALL TOGETHER

Play all parts together. If needed, start with the hands then, add the bass drum.

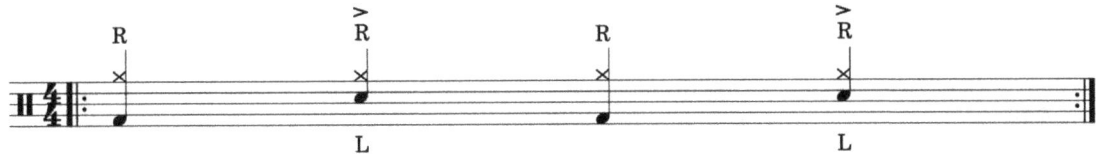

PRO TIP

Keep the hi-hat low and be sure to accent 2 & 4, as this is the essence of the groove. To really stress the upbeats, you can accent the second beat on both the hi-hat and snare. As you develop the chops to play the country groove faster, be sure to stay relaxed, as this rhythm should feel light.

WATCH IT

Find my Country drum groove video at:

https://www.youtube.com/watch?v=QSUWkGONqwU&t=8s

COUNTRY: RHYTHMIC VARIATIONS

COUNTRY ROCK: "MONEY BEAT"

OLD TIME TRAIN BEAT

COUNTRY BALLAD

ELEVATING THE GROOVE

TRAIN BEAT WITH HI-HAT

COUNTRY BALLAD HYBRID

HALFTIME GROOVE

THE GROOVE

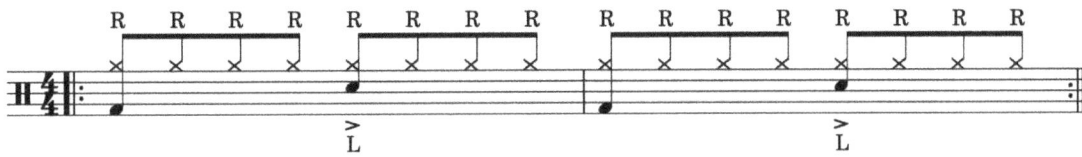

ABOUT IT

This groove is used in a variety styles to include pop, rock, country, and other genres. The essence of the halftime groove is that it gives the song a laidback feel. It is also the primary groove used in ballads in almost every style. Rhythmically, it is an excellent way to add variety to any song because the change in style from standard time (like a rock groove) to halftime provides needed contrast in the music.

LISTEN TO IT
- *What Hurts the Most* by Rascal Flats
- *The Weekend* by SZA
- *Black* by Pearl Jam

LEARN IT: BREAKDOWN

STEP 1: ONE HAND

Start by playing straight eighth notes on the hi-hat with your right hand.

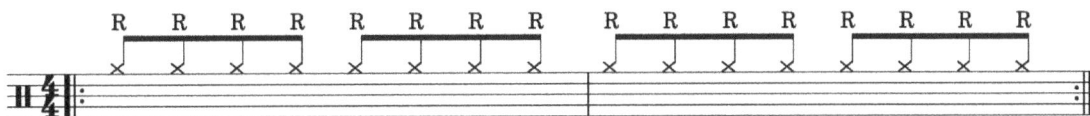

STEP 2: TWO HANDS

Second, add the snare drum on beat 3 with the left hand.

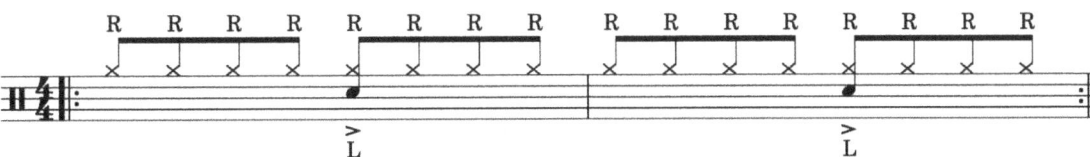

STEP 3: BASS & CYMBAL

Just play the hi-hat and bass drum together. The bass drum is played with the hi-hat on beat one.

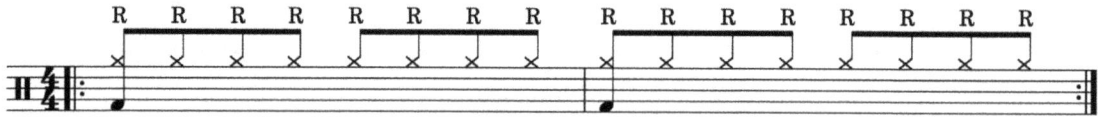

STEP 4: ALL TOGETHER

Now, put all three parts together

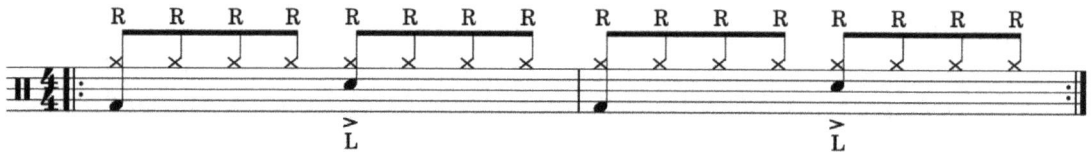

PRO TIP

Be sure to really dig into the accentuated snare drum on beat 3, as this is the part that brings out the halftime feel. Also, you can use a cross stick on the snare to generate a less aggressive percussive effect.

WATCH IT

Find my Halftime drum groove video at:

https://www.youtube.com/watch?v=9Omcv2Gjl0Y&t=14s

HALFTIME: RHYTHMIC VARIATIONS

HALF-TIME ROCK/POP

HALF-TIME ROCK/POP

HALF-TIME ROCK/POP

ELEVATING THE GROOVE

LIFTED HI-HAT W/THREES

HALF-TIME ROCK/POP

CLASSIC POPULAR GROOVES

SURF

THE GROOVE

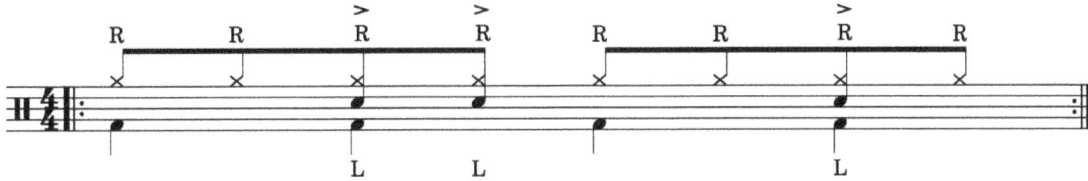

ABOUT IT

Driven by drums and electric guitar, surf music was a genre from Southern California that was popular in the late 1950s and early 1960s. Originally a regional style of rock music, it quickly spread in popularity because of the infectious groove and interest in surf culture throughout the United States. Bands like The Safaris and Beach Boys used the surf groove as the core of their music. The key to this style is the unique backbeat, which is usually played on counts 2, & of 2, and 4.

LISTEN TO IT

- *Wipe Out* by The Safaris
- *Miserlou* by Dick Dale
- *Walk Don't Run* by The Ventures

LEARN IT: BREAKDOWN

STEP 1: ONE HAND

Start with just the cymbal pattern (right hand), which can be played on the hi-hat or ride cymbal. Make sure the eight notes are even (straight eighths).

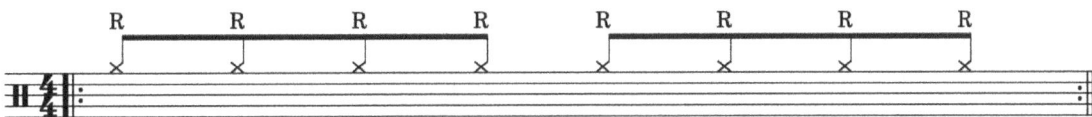

STEP 2: TWO HANDS

Once the cymbal part is steady, add the snare part on 2&, and 4. The best way to approach this is slowly play the right and add the left hand.

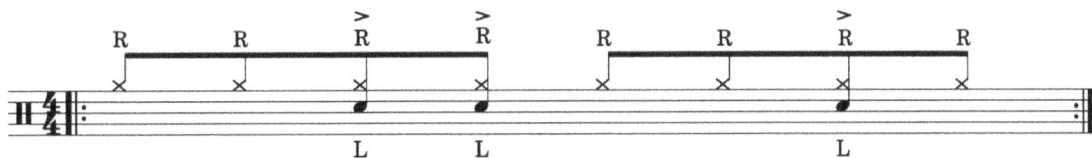

STEP 3: BASS & CYMBAL

Next, play just the bass drum and right hand together. Be sure to make sure they line up.

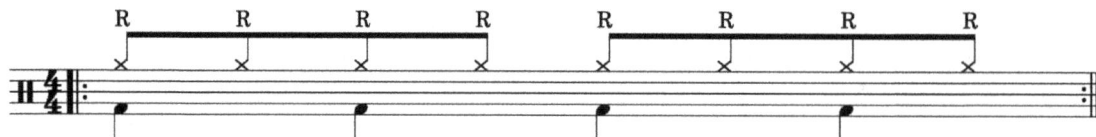

STEP 4: ALL TOGETHER

Last, put all three parts together. Start with the cymbal (right hand), add the snare (left hand), and finally add the bass drum (feet). Once you have this mastered, try starting the groove with all the parts together from the start, but it is okay to layer the patterns at first.

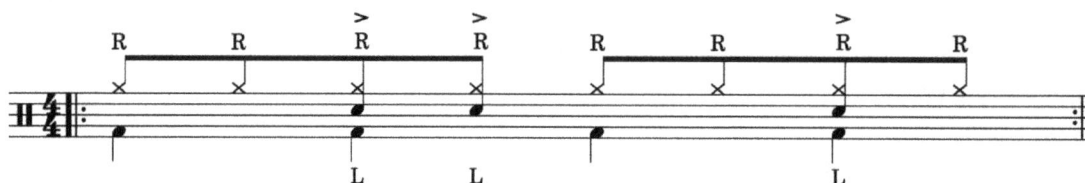

PRO TIP

When playing the snare drum part for this groove, use two different accent volumes for beats 2 and & of 2. Specifically, use a heavier accent on the & of 2, which is more authentic to the style. You will still want a light accent on beat 2, but the upbeat is really the essence of the surf groove.

WATCH IT

Find my Surf Groove video at:

https://www.youtube.com/watch?v=BqqzAuc3dng&t=42s

SURF: RHYTHMIC VARIATIONS

ADDED TOM

HEAVY FLOOR TOM

SURF TOM MIX

ELEVATING THE GROOVE

BASIC SURF WITH LEFT FOOT HI-HAT

HEAVY TOM & FEET

SNARE ON ALL FOUR

THE GROOVE

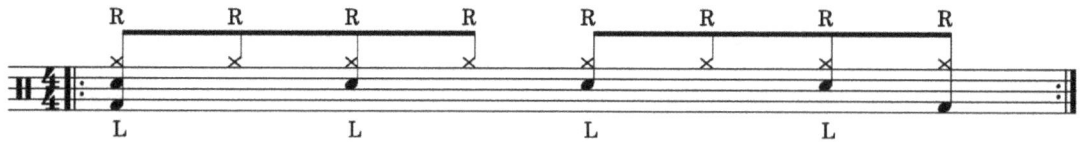

ABOUT IT

One of the best beats to drive a song and add some excitement is the *Snare on All Four Groove*. This rhythm is used in Motown, Punk, Rock, and Pop music. In the 1960s, this groove became the heart and soul of just about every Motown song that was played by the Funk Brothers (the rhythm section that recorded Motown's music). This rhythm adds zest to the music and is a great way to change up a song. Typically, the groove is used during the chorus of a tune to really drive the music.

LISTEN TO IT

- *Reach Out I'll Be There* by The Four Tops
- *Oh, Pretty Women* by Roy Orbison
- *Shout it Out Loud* by KISS

LEARN IT: BREAKDOWN

STEP 1: ONE HAND

Start by playing eighth notes on the hi-hat with the right hand. Use the left hand if you play southpaw.

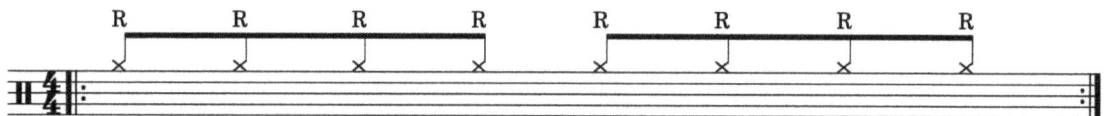

STEP 2: TWO HANDS

Add the snare drum on all four beats: 1, 2, 3, 4. Be sure to play in the center of the head and keep the eighth notes going on the hi-hat.

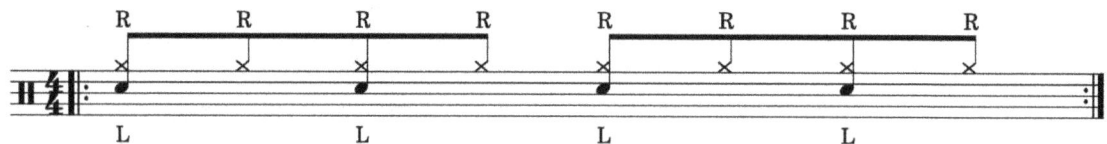

STEP 3: BASS & CYMBAL

Now, play the hi-hat and bass drum together without the snare drum.

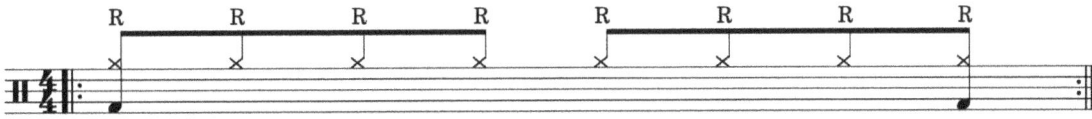

STEP 4: ALL TOGETHER

Play the snare, hi-hat, and bass together. Be sure to start slowly; then once you are comfortable speed up the tempo.

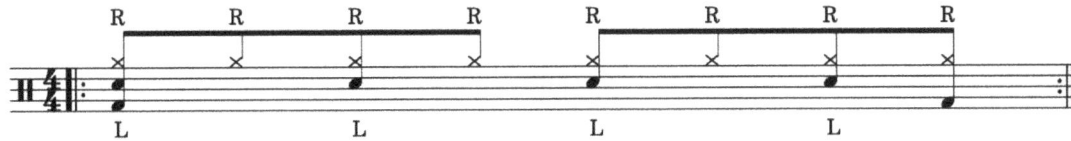

PRO TIP

In some styles, you can add a cross stick on the snare. To do this, place the bead of the stick on the head (about an inch from the rim); then, hit the rim with the thickest part of the drumstick (while keeping the bead on the stick). It should create a crisp knocking sound on the snare.

WATCH IT

Find my Snare on All 4 video at: https://www.youtube.com/watch?v=A6-SzZ5HFOk&t=27s

SNARE ON ALL 4: RHYTHMIC VARIATIONS

UPBEAT BASS

ADDED UPBEAT ON 4

LOTS OF BASS

ELEVATING THE GROOVE

QUICK BASS LICKS

DRIVING HI-HAT

PUNK

THE GROOVE

ABOUT IT

Punk rock drumming is focused on power, speed, and endurance. This style of music is aggressive and driven by the drums. In the mid-1970's underground rock, which would eventually become know as Punk, emerged in clubs in New York (United States), London (England), and Sydney (Australia). In 1976, *Punk Magazine* published articles about these bands and coined the term punk rock, which the creators felt described their attitudes and music itself. Regarding the themes, punk rock tends to focus on non-conformity and working class life. The key to punk drumming is working up the stamina to play quick and powerful eighth notes on the cymbals and successive upbeats on the snare.

LISTEN TO IT
- *Maxwell Murder* by Rancid
- *American Idiot* by Green Day
- *First Date* by Blink 182

LEARN IT: BREAKDOWN

STEP 1: ONE HAND
To begin, play the hi-hat with the right hand.

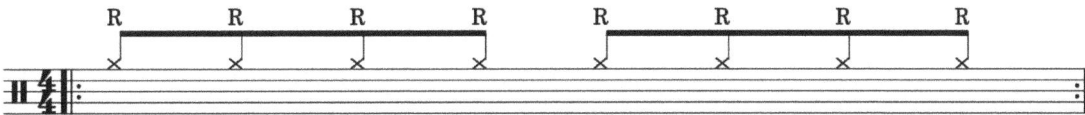

STEP 2: TWO HANDS
Then, add the snare on the up beats

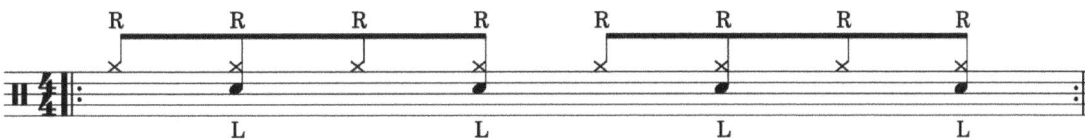

STEP 3: BASS & CYMBAL

Play the hi-hat and bass drum together. The bass drum part is on 1 & 3.

STEP 4: ALL TOGETHER

Put the hi-hat, snare, and bass drum together. But, start with the hi-hat, add the snare, and finally add the bass. Once you have this down, start the groove with all three parts simultaneously and keep it going.

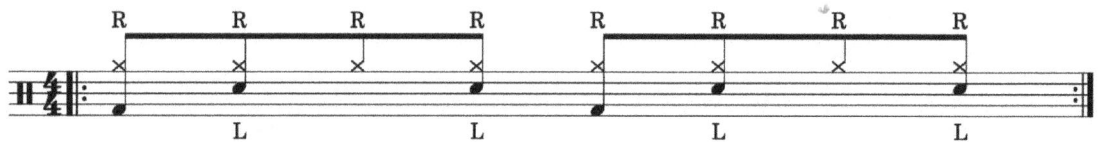

PRO TIP

To really get the punk feel open the hi-hat. The loose hi-hat is commonly used in punk rock and gives the groove a gritty "punk" sound.

WATCH IT

Find my Punk video at: https://www.youtube.com/watch?v=1FyG6s_BNVI&t=5s

PUNK: RHYTHMIC VARIATIONS

BASIC PUNK

HARDCORE PUNK

POP PUNK

ELEVATING THE GROOVE

BUSY PUNK

RIDE & HI-HAT PUNK

DRUM-N-BASS

THE GROOVE

ABOUT IT

Initially, this groove served as the foundation of funk tunes like *Amen, Brother* by The Winstons and *Funky Drummer* by James Brown. These grooves were sampled and eventually played on drum machines like the Roland TR-808. During the 1990s and 2000s, these drum samples became the rhythmic foundation of Drum-N-Bass. In this style, the drums are heavy, busy, and serve as the nucleus this breed of dance music.

LISTEN TO IT
- *Tarantula* by Pendulum
- *Warhead* by Krust
- *Against the Tide* by Delta Heavy

LEARN IT: BREAKDOWN

STEP 1: ONE HAND
Play the eighth notes on the hi-hat with the right hand (left if left handed).

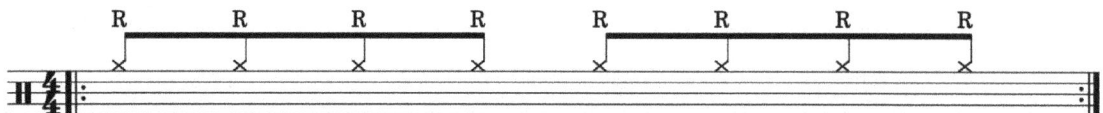

STEP 2: TWO HANDS
Play just the hands, but start by playing the pattern slowly at first. Pay special attention to when the snare and hi-hat are played together (both hands) and when the parts are separate. Be sure to emphasize the accented parts, which occur when the snare and hi-hat are played together.

STEP 3: BASS & CYMBAL
Stop playing the snare part (left hand); then, add the bass drum on one while continuing to play the hi-hat.

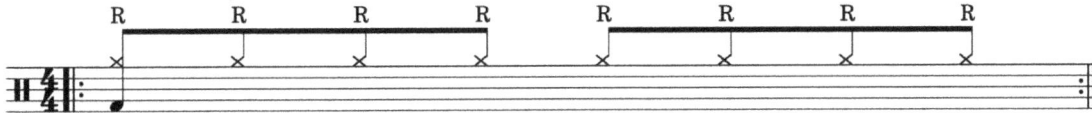

STEP 4: ALL TOGETHER

Play all parts together. If needed, start with the hands then, add the bass drum.

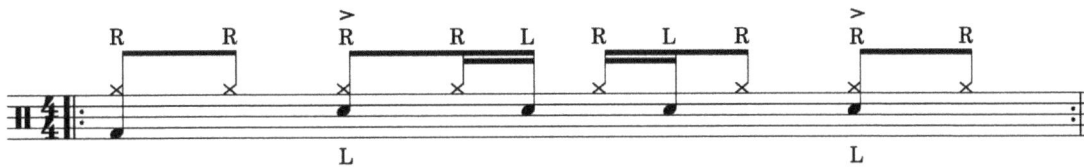

PRO TIP

The non-accented snare notes in this groove should be played as ghost notes (taps), which means that these notes should be gently played on the snare. To make this beat sound epic, dig into the accents and keep the taps low. This will emphasize accents (the essence of the groove) and make you sound like a pro.

WATCH IT

Find my Drum-N-Bass video at:

https://www.youtube.com/watch?v=w1li3V8ZQpE&t=105s

DRUM-N-BASS: RHYTHMIC VARIATIONS

MORE BASS

WARHEAD

HEAVY 16TH NOTE HI-HAT

ELEVATING THE GROOVE

BROKEN SIXTEENTHS

ADD LEFT FOOT

GOSPEL & SOUL

THE GROOVE

ABOUT IT

The backbone of gospel and soul music is the drums, which support the genres powerful vocalists by providing a concrete rhythmic foundation. Gospel music is primarily a style of African American Christian worship music from the Southern United States and Rhythm & Blues. A subgenre of this style is soul music, which sounds very similar, but focuses on dancing and less on the religious aspects. Both styles have a strong emphasis on the vocalist and connecting with the listener. It is the job of the rhythm section (especially the drummer) to provide solid, emotive, and expressive grooves to help convey the message of music.

LISTEN TO IT

- *His Love* by The Clark Sisters
- *Still by* Brian Courtney Wilson
- *I Can't Give Up* by Byron Cage (Shout Groove)

LEARN IT: BREAKDOWN

STEP 1: ONE HAND

Start by playing just the eighth notes with the right hand on the hi-hat. Use you left hand if you are a left-handed player.

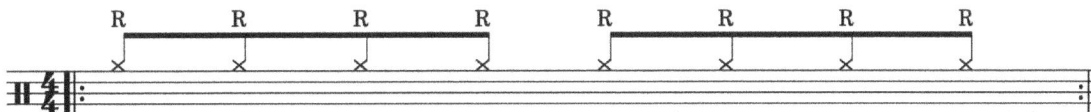

STEP 2: TWO HANDS

Now add a cross stick snare drum on 2 & 4 using you left hand (reverse if you're a lefty)

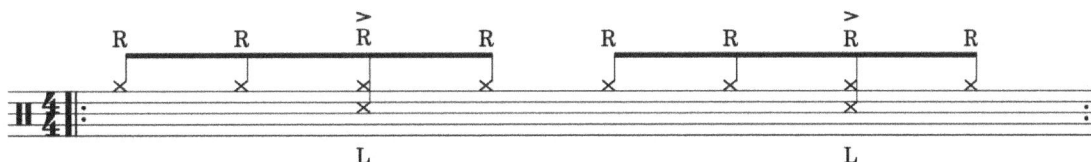

STEP 3: BASS & CYMBAL

Keep the hi-hat going and add the bass drum on 1 & 3. Then, add the pick-up sixteenth note before 3. Start by playing this slowly, and then speed it up.

STEP 4: ALL TOGETHER

Slowly play all three parts together. Once you are comfortable with the groove, you can increase the tempo, but this music is not usually too quick. Be sure to accent 2 & 4 on the snare drum.

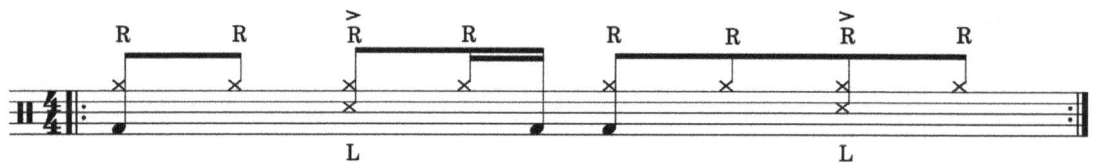

PRO TIP

Since the purpose of this rhythm is to get the listener to really feel the music, this groove should be played on the backside of the beat. This means that you will want to play the rhythms, especially the snare, a little behind the beat. This is a subtle idea, but essential in getting the correct feel.

WATCH IT

Find my Gospel & Soul video at:

https://www.youtube.com/watch?v=TloyOrBl6gE

GOSPEL & SOUL: RHYTHMIC VARIATIONS

HALFTIME 16THS

THE SHOUT

R&B FEEL

ELEVATING THE GROOVE

OFF SET SNARE

OFF SET SNARE WITH UPBEAT HI-HAT

R&B TRIPLET GROOVE

THE GROOVE

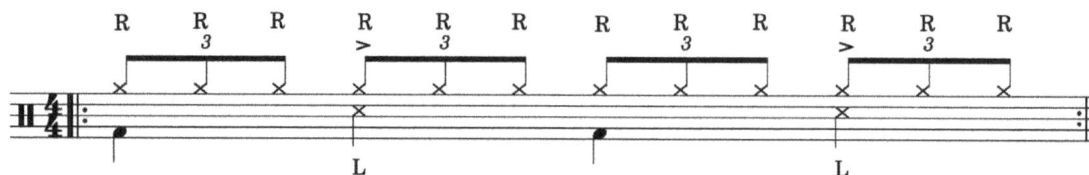

ABOUT IT

The *R&B Triplet Groove* is used in Soul, R&B, and Contemporary R&B. This groove has been used in Rhythm & Blues since the late 1940s and was popularized by musicians like Fats Domino in the 1950s, who used triplets on the piano that were accompanied his drummer (Cornelius "Tenoo" Coleman). The key to getting the right feel on the *R&B Triplet Groove* is to layback on the beat. This can be heard in the music of Etta James, Gladys Knight, and others.

LISTEN TO IT

- *At Last* by Etta James
- *Blueberry Hill* by Fats Domino
- *Every Beat of My Heart* by Gladys Knight
- *Sure Thing by* Miguel

LEARN IT: BREAKDOWN

STEP 1: ONE HAND

Play the triplet pattern on the hi-hat with the right hand. Or, left hand if you are left handed.

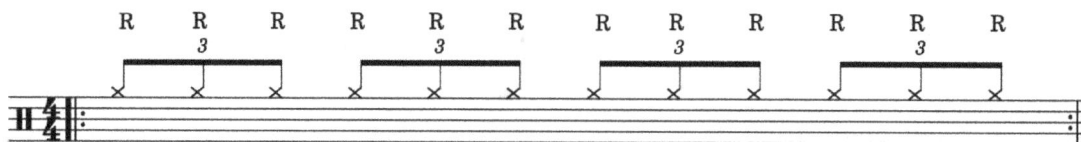

STEP 2: TWO HANDS

Add the snare drum, which should be played with the left hand as a cross stick on 2 and 4. This is known as the *backbeat* and needs to be emphasized. See *Pro Tip* below on how to play a good cross stick.

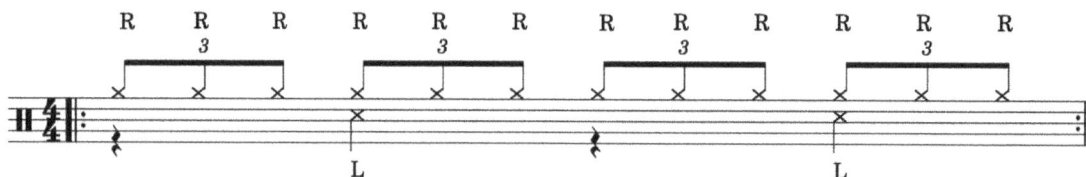

54

STEP 3: BASS & CYMBAL

Keep the hi-hat triplets going and add the bass drum on 1 & 3.

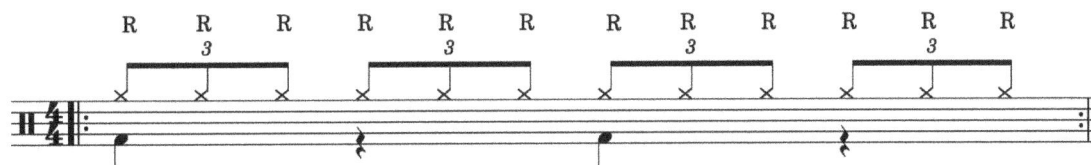

STEP 4: ALL TOGETHER

Put it all together. First, play the hi-hat part. Second, add the cross stick on the snare drum. Last, add the bass drum. Once you can get the groove going; stop, and play it all together without layering the parts.

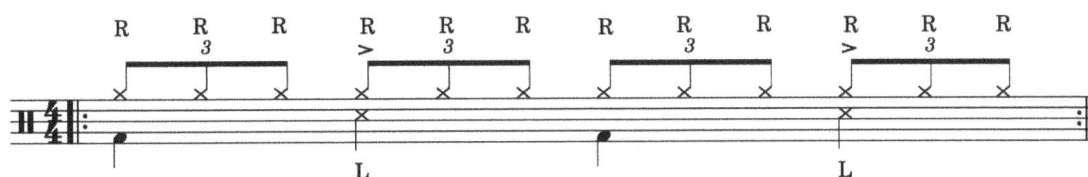

PRO TIP

To get an awesome cross stick on the snare, you will need to flip the stick over. Then, place the bead of the stick on the head about an inch from the rim. With a lever motion (keeping the bead on the drum head and holding the stick), hit the rim with the shaft of the stick (toward the back) on the rim. This should give you a crisp click. For more info here is a video on how to play a cross stick:

https://www.youtube.com/watch?v=lFC1-6BmM7c

WATCH IT

Find my video at: https://www.youtube.com/watch?v=qGM3KwCObDE&t=62s

R&B TRIPLET GROOVE: RHYTHMIC VARIATIONS

BOOM BOOM

LITTLE EXTRA SNARE

ADD THREE

ELEVATING THE GROOVE

FUNKY OFF BEAT HI-HAT

SOUL WITH THREES

REGGAE

THE GROOVE

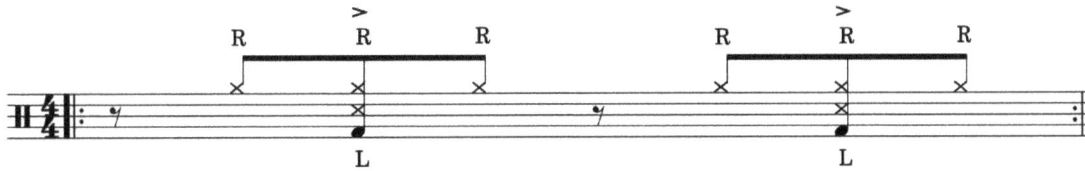

ABOUT IT

Reggae is a musical style from Jamaica, which uses the rock steady beat. This groove can be described as "rock music turned upside down" because the bass drum occurs on the backbeat (2 & 4). This small change gives the rhythm a completely different feel. The predecessor of reggae is Jamaican ska, which was a fusion of 1950s rock and calypso grooves. Reggae emerged in the late 1960s as a protest music regarding social conditions in Jamaica. The infectious rhythms and message quickly became popular throughout the world with artists like Bob Marley and Peter Tosh

LISTEN TO IT

- *Is This Love* by Bob Marley & The Wailers
- *Legalize It* by Peter Tosh
- *The Harder They Come by* Jimmy Cliff

LEARN IT: BREAKDOWN

STEP 1: ONE HAND

Play the hi-hat pattern in the right hand (left hand if you are a lefty).

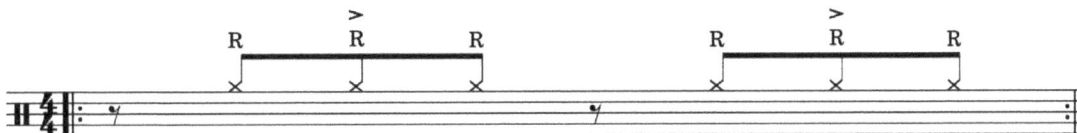

STEP 2: TWO HANDS

Add the bass drum, which is played on 2 & 4. Be sure to accent 2 & 4 in the hi-hat when playing the bass.

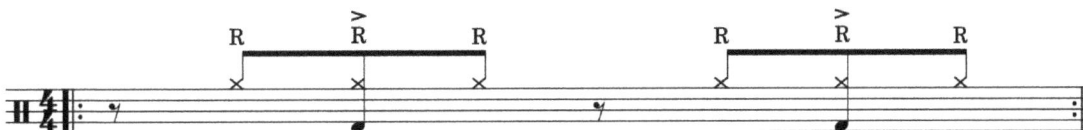

STEP 3: HANDS ONLY

Play just the hi-hat and cross stick on the snare.

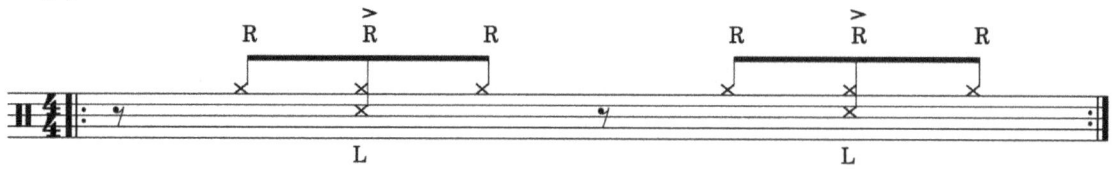

STEP 4: HANDS ONLY

Finally, put all three parts together. Be sure to keep a heavy accent on beats 2 & 4.

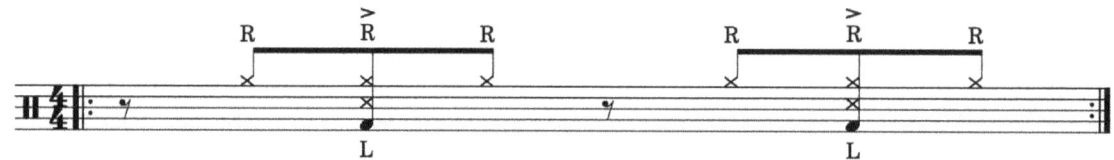

<table>
<tr><td>PRO TIP</td></tr>
</table>

PRO TIP

Since this everything in this groove is the reverse of pop and rock grooves, take some time to master playing bass on 2 & 4. In addition, try to lay back when playing the reggae groove, which means to play a little behind the beat.

WATCH IT

Find my reggae video at: https://www.youtube.com/watch?v=DhFK-qTut_s&t=8s

REGGAE: RHYTHMIC VARIATIONS

ONE DROP

SYNCOPATED REGGAE

TRIPLET REGGAE

ELEVATING THE GROOVE

ONE DROP W/OFF BEAT HI-HAT

BUSY TRIPLET REGGAE

WALTZ

THE GROOVE

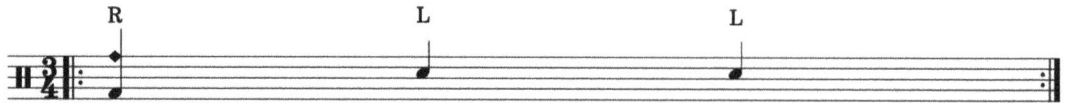

ABOUT IT

The waltz is a dance groove that is derived from European classical music. It is essential for playing drums in musicals, ballroom dances, Mexican cumbia, and other styles. The basic rhythm is easy to play and requires only a few embellishments. The key to making the waltz sound good is to accent beat one, as this is emphasized in the dance and dancers will expect to feel a strong downbeat.

LISTEN TO IT

- *Come Away With Me* by Norah Jones
- *Embassy Waltz* by Andre Previn (from *My Fair Lady*)
- *Skaters Waltz* by Émile Waldteufel

LEARN IT: BREAKDOWN

STEP 1: ONE HAND

Play just the cymbal and snare drum using the following pattern: R L L. While using this sticking, count each beat (1, 2, 3).

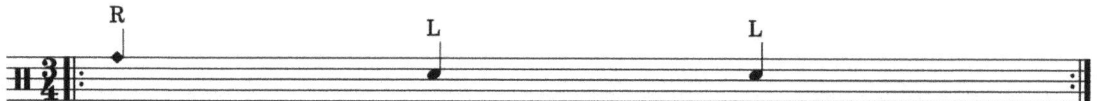

STEP 2: TWO HANDS

Next, play the bass drum (B) and snare drum (S), which is B S S. I suggest using the following sticking B L L.

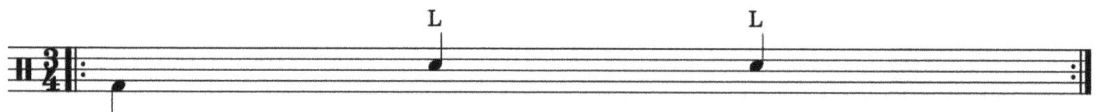

STEP 3: ALL TOGETHER
Finally, put all three parts together and be sure to emphasize the first beat.

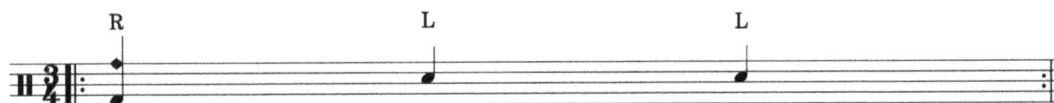

PRO TIP

Since this is dance music, be sure to keep the groove light. It is best to have a gentle touch, while still stressing the downbeat. To do this, keep any improvisations minimal and play snare drum gently and softer than the bass/cymbal parts.

WATCH IT
Find my Waltz video at: https://www.youtube.com/watch?v=fo7olWSSc5w

WALTZ: RHYTHMIC VARIATIONS

WALTZ WITH HI-HAT

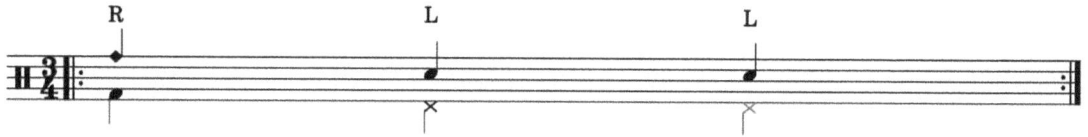

HALF-TIME ROCK/POP

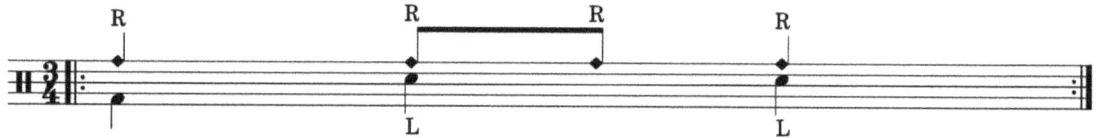

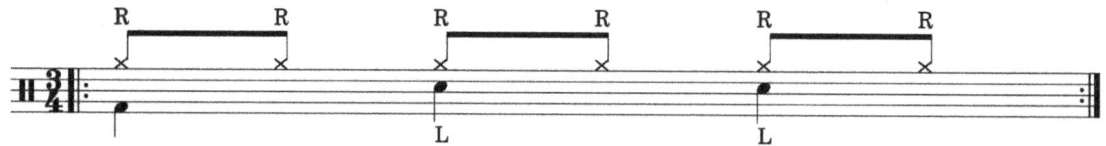

HALF-TIME ROCK/POP

ELEVATING THE GROOVE

LIFTED HI-HAT W/THREES

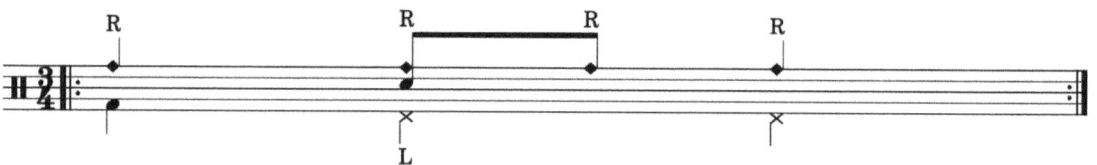

LIFTED HI-HAT W/THREES

SWING & SHUFFLE GROOVES

SHUFFLE

THE GROOVE

ABOUT IT

The shuffle is a classic groove that serves as the rhythmic foundation of the blues, rock, funk, hip-hop, swing, and some country music. This beat is the predecessor of straight eighth rhythm used in rock music. A good way to get the feel of this groove is to play the rock/pop groove; then, put a bit more space between the beats (making it swing). If you do that, you will be playing a shuffle.

LISTEN TO IT

- *Paying the Cost to Be the Boss* by B.B. King
- *Revolution* by The Beatles
- *Rock this Town* by Brian Setzer Orchestra or The Stray Cats

LEARN IT: BREAKDOWN

STEP 1: ONE HAND
To learn this groove, start with the hi-hat (right hand). The key is to let the "shuffle" rhythm feel like it bounces.

STEP 2: TWO HANDS
Once this is mastered, add the snare drum on 2 & 4, which is the part that makes people want to dance.

STEP 3: BASS & CYMBAL

Play the hi-hat and bass drum parts together. The bass drum should be played lightly and serves as the pulse of the groove.

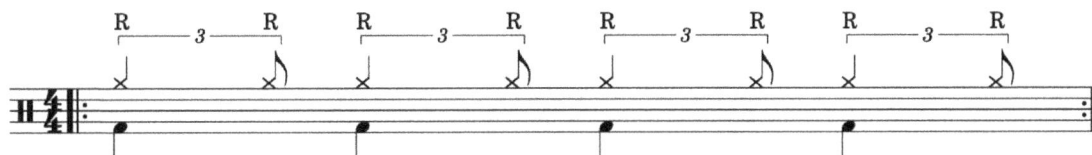

STEP 4: ALL TOGETHER

Now, play all three parts together. Once you are comfortable with the groove, you can increase the tempo. Be sure to keep the shuffle feel.

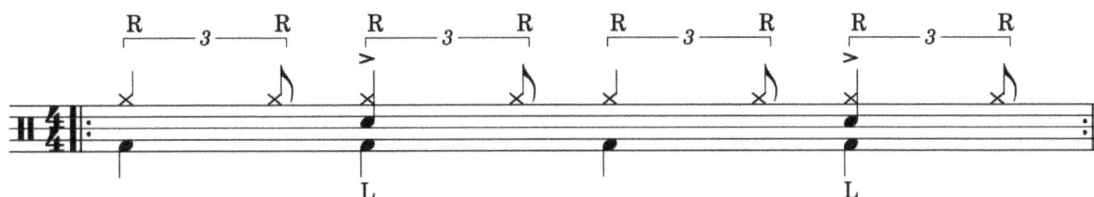

PRO TIP

Heavily accent the snare drum because this is the most important part of the groove. Also, try the bass drum at different volumes, as different shuffle styles require the bass drum to be played gently, moderately, or aggressively.

WATCH IT

Find my Shuffle video at: https://www.youtube.com/watch?v=8_RYTpgh6vE

SHUFFLE: RHYTHMIC VARIATIONS

FUNK SHUFFLE

ROCKABILLY SHUFFLE

Play snare clicks on the rim and accented notes on the head.

ROCKABILLY SHUFFLE

ELEVATING THE GROOVE

CLASSIC SHUFFLE W/HI-HAT

"PHAT" LEFT HAND SHUFFLE

SWING

THE GROOVE

w/Left Foot

ABOUT IT

The soul of traditional jazz, big band, and straight-ahead jazz is the swing groove. In the early 1900s this stemmed from "ragging" the beat by street drummers in New Orleans, which meant to make the groove swing. In the 1930s and 1940s, this groove was the core of big band jazz, which was popular dance music. The key to playing this rhythm is accenting 2 and 4; plus, making the ride cymbal bounce/swing. Please note: This is the basic swing groove. To play jazz requires a few more elements, but every jazz drummer starts with this.

LISTEN TO IT

- *It Don't Mean a Thing if it Ain't Got That Swing* by Duke Ellington
- *Moanin'* by Art Blakey
- *One O'clock Jump* by Count Basie

LEARN IT: BREAKDOWN

STEP 1: ONE HAND

Before adding the bass drum and hi-hat, which is played with the foot, I recommend mastering the ride (right hand) pattern. This is the soul of the swing groove. Specifically, accent 2 and 4 with the ride, as this provides the proper feel.

STEP 2: TWO HANDS

Once this is grasped, add the left foot (hi-hat). This will stress 2 and 4 even more. Oh, be sure to keep the accents on the ride.

STEP 3: BASS & CYMBAL

Now, play just the bass drum (lightly) and ride cymbal pattern. Again, be sure to accent 2 and 4.

STEP 4: ALL TOGETHER

Last, put all three parts together.

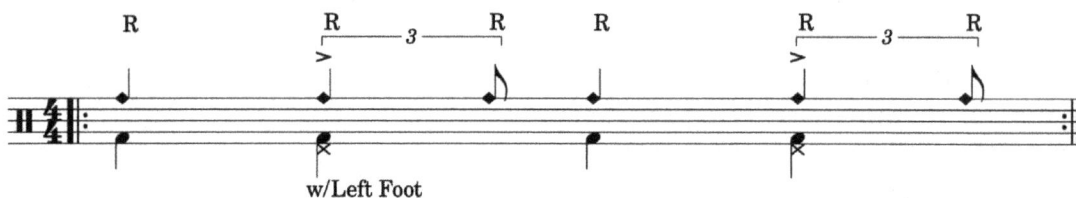

w/Left Foot

PRO TIP

When playing the bass drum it is best to *feather it*, which means to play it very delicately. In this style, the ride cymbal is the essence, as it is the drummer's job to create the feel of the song. The bass drum simply supports the groove by playing a "walking bass line," which is played by on an upright (traditional) or electric bass.

WATCH IT

Find my Swing video at: https://www.youtube.com/watch?v=TAXip-d-BLw

SWING: RHYTHMIC VARIATIONS

CROSS STICK ON 4

TWO BEAT

SYNCOPATED UPBEAT

ELEVATING THE GROOVE

HEMIOLA STYLE

TRIPLET & CLICK

JAZZ WALTZ

THE GROOVE

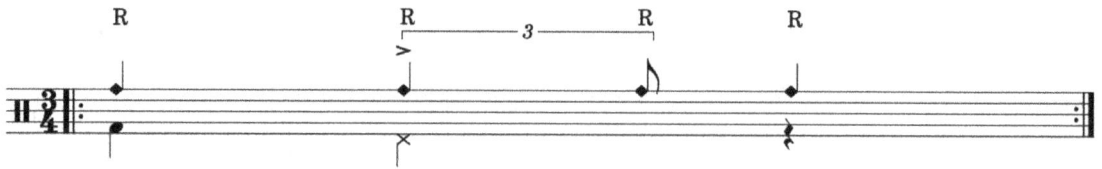

ABOUT IT

The jazz waltz is a groove that every jazz drummer needs in his or her rhythmic arsenal. In the late 1950s and early 1960s jazz combos were fusing a variety of styles into the genre, which included waltzes. Originally a dance style used in classical music., but the key to playing a jazz waltz is the swing feel. Like a standard swing rhythm, which accents 2 and 4, the jazz waltz requires an emphasis on 2, as there is no fourth beat.

LISTEN TO IT

- *The Drum Also Waltzes* by Max Roach
- *All Blues* by Miles Davis
- *Footprints* by Wayne Shorter

LEARN IT: BREAKDOWN

STEP 1: ONE HAND

Play the swing pattern on the ride cymbal with the right hand (switch to the left if you are left handed). Be sure to accent the second beat.

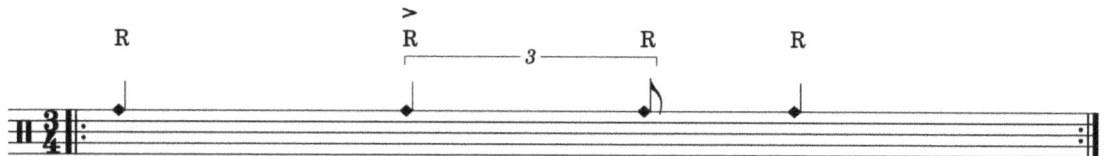

STEP 2: TWO HANDS

Add the hi-hat with your foot on beat 2. Be sure that this lines up with the accented note on the ride cymbal.

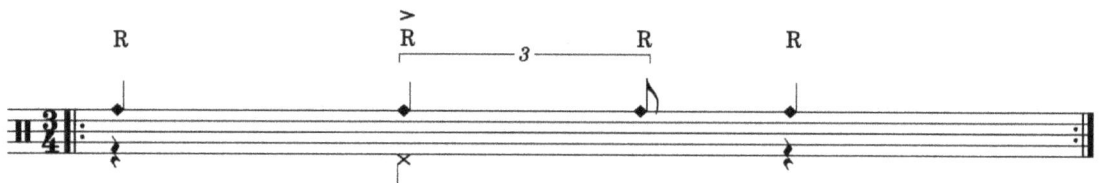

70

STEP 3: BASS & CYMBAL

Continue playing the ride cymbal and the bass drum on the down beat (beat 1).

STEP 4: ALL TOGETHER

Now, put all three parts together. Since this groove requires both feet, focus on keeping your core stable by sitting at the edge of the drum throne (seat) and sitting up straight.

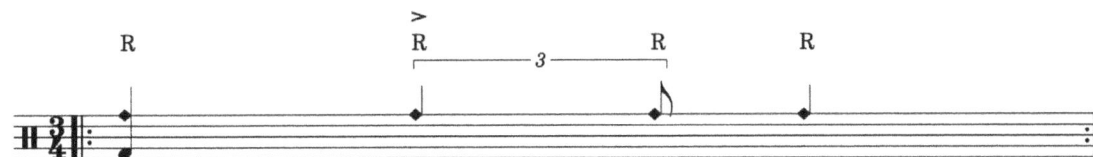

PRO TIP

Spend a good amount of time mastering the ride cymbal part for this groove, as nothing is more important to get the right feel. Once you have it down, it will serve as the foundation of the groove and allow you to freely experiment with the left hand.

WATCH IT

Find my Jazz Waltz video at:

https://www.youtube.com/watch?v=4KiSq4OJcng&t=48s

JAZZ WALTZ: RHYTHMIC VARIATIONS

ONE UP BEAT

TWO UP BEATS

VIENNESE STYLE

ELEVATING THE GROOVE

TRIPLET CITY

LEADING TO ONE

SECOND-LINE

THE GROOVE

ABOUT IT

Originally played on the streets of New Orleans (USA), second line drumming is a funky "ragged" (term used in the early 1900s) groove that was used to accompany brass bands in the early 1900s. Overtime, second-line rhythms were played on marching drums (snare, bass drum, cymbals) and used by early jazz drummers. Second-line drumming has its own unique lineage, heavily influenced jazz drummers, and can still be heard on the streets of New Orleans today. The essence of this groove is the shuffle pattern and clave, which give it a swung and syncopated feel.

LISTEN TO IT

- *Hey Pocky A-Way* by The Meters
- *It Must Have Been Ol' Santa Claus* by Harry Connick Jr
- *When the Saint's Go Marching In by* Funky 7 Brass Band or any other New Orleans brass band.

LEARN IT: BREAKDOWN

STEP 1: CLAVE

Start by playing the clave pattern. Be sure to use the sticking below, as this will be important when combining the shuffle pattern and accents in Step 3.

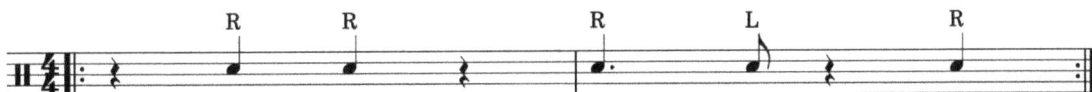

STEP 2: TWO HANDS

Play just the shuffle pattern, which should have a swung or "ragged" feel to it. Get the feel of this rhythm down before adding the accents in Step 3.

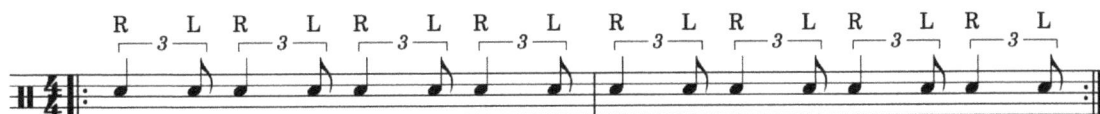

STEP 3: ACCENTS

Keep the shuffle pattern going, but now add the clave pattern accents. Keep the non-accented notes (taps or ghost notes) low, as this will allow the accented notes to pop.

STEP 4: ALL TOGETHER

Last, add the bass drum on one while playing the syncopated snare pattern.

PRO TIP

To make your second line groove sound authentic, you can add the hi-hat (with your foot) on 2 and 4. A transcription of this version of the groove can be found in the Elevating the Groove section on the next page. Of course, be sure to keep the accents up and the taps (ghost notes) low, as this will maintain the proper feel.

WATCH IT

Find my Second-Line video at:

https://www.youtube.com/watch?v=omsZajZXJt8&t=24s

SECOND-LINE: RHYTHMIC VARIATIONS

3:2 SECOND-LINE

TWO-BEAT STYLE

MARCH STYLE

ELEVATING THE GROOVE

3:2 SECOND-LINE WITH HI-HAT

2:3 SECOND-LINE LINE WITH HI-HAT

LATIN GROOVES

CHA-CHA

THE GROOVE

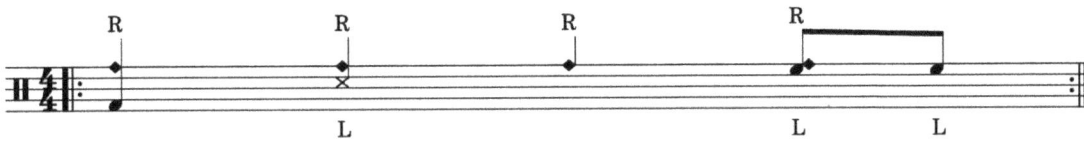

ABOUT IT

The *cha-cha*, which is also known as the *cha-cha-cha*, is a dance groove that can be heard in Latin, pop, rock, and country music. The rhythm has Cuban origins and was derived from the mambo in the 1950s. While it was initially a form of popular dance music, the *cha-cha* has become standard repertoire in ballroom dancing. The key to playing this groove is the interplay between driving quarter and conga pattern, which can be substituted by the ride cymbal bell (cowbell) and cross stick snare with tom (conga) on the drum set.

LISTEN TO IT

- *Oye Como Va* by Tito Puente (original) or Santana
- *Besame Mama* by Pancho Sanchez
- *My Maria* by Brooks & Dunn

LEARN IT: BREAKDOWN

STEP 1: ONE HAND

Start by playing steady quarter notes on the ride cymbal or cowbell (if you have one).

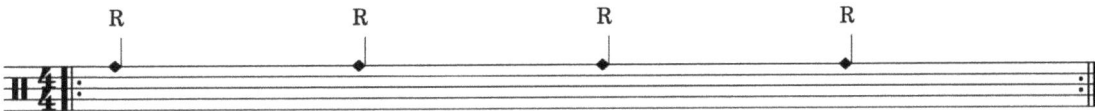

STEP 2: TWO HANDS

Next, add the snare and high tom pattern by playing a cross stick on the snare on two and a eighth notes on beats 4& on the tom. This simulates the slap and open tones.

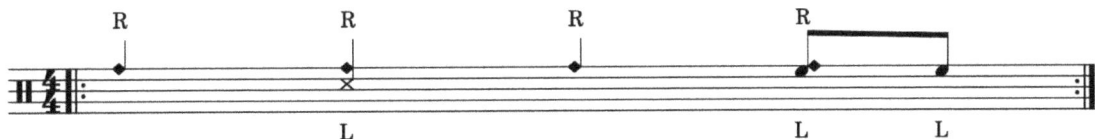

STEP 3: BASS & CYMBAL

Play just ride cymbal and add the bass drum on beat one.

STEP 4: ALL TOGETHER

Finally, put all three parts together to create this dance groove.

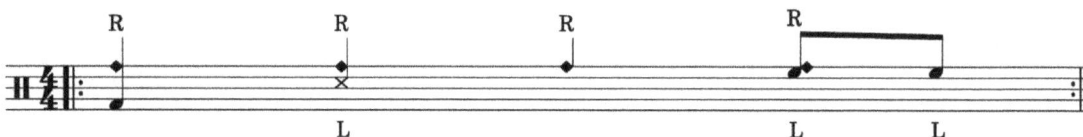

PRO TIP

The *cha-cha* has a lot of open space because it is does not rely on steady eighth notes to fill on the gap like many other beats, which makes it easy to rush. When playing the groove, it is best to keep the quarter notes open and steady. When practicing, use a metronome and when playing with others, be sure to stay on the backside of the beat.

WATCH IT

Find my Cha-Cha video at:

https://www.youtube.com/watch?v=tM2ttm4D5Ss&t=25s

CHA-CHA: RHYTHMIC VARIATIONS

DRIVING EIGHTHS CHA-CHA

SNARE ON EVERY BEAT

CONGA & TUMBA STYLE

ELEVATING THE GROOVE

DRIVING EIGHTHS CHA-CHA W/LEFT FOOT

CONGA & CLAVE STYLE W/LEFT FOOT

SAMBA

THE GROOVE

ABOUT IT

Traditionally played on the streets of Rio de Janeiro, the samba is a high-energy syncopated groove that makes people dance. At Carnival in Brazil, hundreds of drummers will form a samba school and play on traditional instruments, such as the surdo, caixa, timbal, and pandeiro. As a collective, each section of the ensemble has their own unique rhythms that create the polyrhythms used in Brazilian samba. On the drum set, the samba can be recreated (though simplified from the original) by emphasizing key patterns. For example, the surdo pattern (large drum) is played on the bass drum. These drum set patterns are commonly used on Latin jazz tunes. The key to playing this groove is keeping the bass drum and cymbal part light, while emphasizing the snare.

LISTEN TO IT

- *Mas Que Nada* by Sergio Mendez
- *Quem Quieir Encontrar O Amor* by Tamba Trio
- *Spain by Chick Corea*

LEARN IT: BREAKDOWN

STEP 1: ONE HAND

With the right hand (or left if you're a lefty), play the three-note rhythm on the ride cymbal or hi-hat.

STEP 2: TWO HANDS

Play the Brazilian clave in the left hand (cross stick). Then, play it slowly with the cymbal pattern. Take your time, as you will really want master this before moving on.

STEP 3: BASS & CYMBAL

Now, play just the bass drum; then, play the bass drum pattern with the cymbal. Again, you will want to master this rhythm so that it becomes automatic.

STEP 4: ALL TOGETHER

Last, put all three parts together. To do this, keep the bass drum and cymbal pattern going; then, add each snare hit note by note. .

PRO TIP

To play a samba like a pro, keep the groove light and smooth. This groove is designed for dancing and should flow under the melody. Also, if you put accents on the 1 & 2 (remember this is in cut time) in the ride and bass drum, it gives the groove the perfect feel.

WATCH IT

Find my Samba video at:
https://www.youtube.com/watch?v=AxcVxZkkkBE&t=54s

SAMBA: RHYTHMIC VARIATIONS

EASY SAMBA (AKA: CHEATER SAMBA)

SNARE SAMBA

TRADITIONAL SAMBA

ELEVATING THE GROOVE

JAZZ SAMBA (EASY)

LINEAR SAMBA

BOSSA NOVA

THE GROOVE

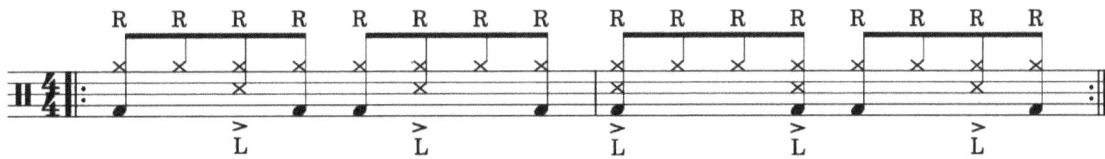

ABOUT IT

The *bossa nova,* or "new beat," is a smooth and laid back Brazilian groove that was originally played by guitarists Antônio Carlos Jobim and João Gilberto. In many ways, the *bossa nova* is a simplified samba that developed into its own style. The jazz drummer Milton Banana (Antônio de Souza) is considered the fist to apply this groove to drum set, which he incorporated into his playing with jazz musician Stan Getz and João Gilberto. This groove is typically associated with the cool jazz movement in the 1960s. The essence of the *bossa nova* drum groove is the repeated bass drum pattern (ostinato) and *clave,* which is played with a cross stick on the snare.

LISTEN TO IT
- *The Girl from Impanema* by Antonio Carlos Jobim and Frank Sinatra
- *Corcovada* by Stan Getz & João Gilberto
- *Blue Bossa* by Joe Henderson

LEARN IT: BREAKDOWN

STEP 1: ONE HAND

Start by playing steady eighth notes on the hi-hat (right hand), which can be played with the left if you are a lefty.

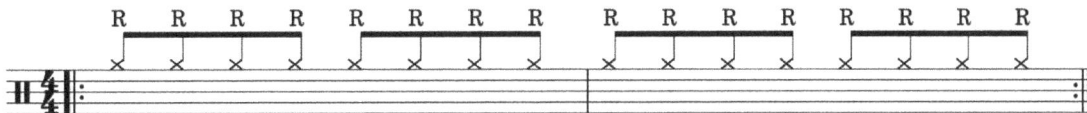

STEP 2: TWO HANDS

Keep the hi-hat going. Now, add the cross stick on the snare. One suggestion is to play one note, then two, then three, and so on.

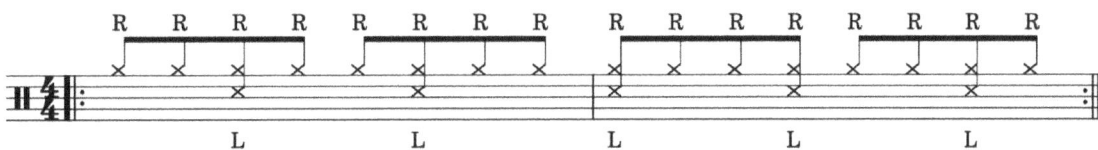

STEP 3: BASS & CYMBAL

Stop playing the snare part (left hand), but keep the hi-hat (right hand) going. Add the repeated rhythm on the bass drum. Keep this light, as it is not a heavy groove.

STEP 4: ALL TOGETHER

Now slowly put all three parts together, but start with just the hi-hat and bass drum. Then once the groove is set, add the clave.

PRO TIP

When playing the *bossa nova* keep the rhythms light, but driving. This groove is traditionally laid back, played with guitarist, and a designed to support vocalist/soloist. I always keep this is mind when playing the *bossa nova*.

WATCH IT

Find my Bossa Nova video at:
https://www.youtube.com/watch?v=3NLKATkSWgw&t=33s

BOSSA NOVA: RHYTHMIC VARIATIONS

ADD TOMS

FLIPPED BOSSA

DRESSED UP BOSSA

ELEVATING THE GROOVE

ADDING LEFT FOOT HI-HAT

LOTS OF HI-HAT

CALYPSO/SOCA

THE GROOVE

ABOUT IT

Derived from West African drumming, calypso and soca rhythms are played in pop music, steel drum bands, and traditional music in Trinidad and Tobago. Many bands will use drum set; however, hand drums and shakers are also common, as the drum set rhythms stem from traditional drumming. The essence of this groove is the driving syncopated rhythm in the bass drum and snare. This is a fun rhythm to play, but it takes a good amount of practice to get the hang of.

LISTEN TO IT

- *Jean &* Dinah by Mighty Sparrow
- *Hot Hot Hot* by Buster Poindexter
- *Day-O* by Harry Belafonte

LEARN IT: BREAKDOWN

STEP 1: ONE HAND

Start by playing just the hi-hat patter with the right hand, which is RRR. Play it slow at fist then speed it up.

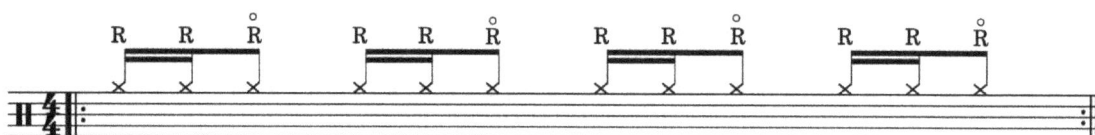

STEP 2: TWO HANDS

Next, add the snare drum part, which occurs between the first two sets of threes (RRR) and the last beat. So, it looks like this RRRL RRT. The "T" means to play both hands together.

STEP 3: BASS & CYMBAL

Now, play the bass drum on 1 & 3 while playing the cymbal part.

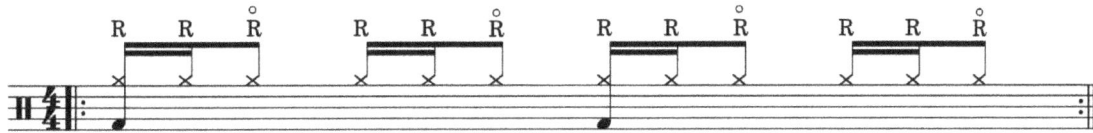

STEP 4: ALL TOGETHER

Finally, put all three parts together. Pay special attention to the syncopated rhythm that is played between the bass and snare drum underneath the hi-hat.

PRO TIP

Once you have mastered the basic sticking there is an open hi-hat that occurs on the upbeats. To make this pop, I suggest putting a little accent on the upbeat.

WATCH IT

Find my Calypso/Soca video at:

https://www.youtube.com/watch?v=1N1SB9pEmUY&t=15s

CALYPSO/SOCA: RHYTHMIC VARIATIONS

OPEN HI-HAT

STEADY EIGHTHS CALYPSO

HEMIOLA SOCA

ELEVATING THE GROOVE

RIDE AND HI-HAT COMBO

UPBEAT HI-HAT CALYPSO

MAMBO

THE GROOVE

ABOUT IT

The mambo is a syncopated, catchy, and danceable groove that is the cornerstone of Cuban music. Traditionally, the percussion parts are played on timbales, congas, and claves. This version of the groove is a variation created for drum set. Initially, mambo was popularized in Cuba in the 1930s, but quickly became popular in the United States, Mexico, and other countries. The most important elements of the mambo are the following: (1) Clave pattern, which is played as a snare drum cross stick; (2) Cascara, which is played on the ride bell, but it traditionally played on the shell of a timbale. In any case, this is a fun dance groove to play and something every drummer should know.

LISTEN TO IT
- *Mambo Inn* by Tito Puente
- *Mambo No. 5* by Perez Prado or Lou Bega
- *Mambo Italiano* by Dean Martin

LEARN IT: BREAKDOWN

STEP 1: ONE HAND

Begin by playing the syncopated *cascara* pattern on the ride bell with your right hand. Use the left if you are left-handed.

STEP 2: TWO HANDS

Add the clave pattern with the left hand (right for left handed players) on the snare drum using a cross stick (this simulates the clave). Take this slow, as it takes practice and patience to master the combined rhythms.

STEP 3: BASS & CYMBAL
Play the bass drum on beat one while playing the cascara pattern on the ride bell.

STEP 4: ALL TOGETHER
Last, slowly put all three parts together and speed it up, once it is comfortable.

PRO TIP
The most important part of this groove is the clave; so, be sure that the clave pattern (cross stick snare) pops when playing the other parts. Also, you can play the ride bell pattern (cascara) on the rim, which gives it a dryer more authentic sound. Plus, it helps the clave pop, which is key to playing this rhythm.

WATCH IT
Find my Mambo video at:
https://www.youtube.com/watch?v=ioLAPp6PSnk&t=8s

MAMBO: RHYTHMIC VARIATIONS

ADD CONGA

2:3 CLAVE W/BASS

3:2 CLAVE

ELEVATING THE GROOVE

2:3 CLAVE W/BASS

CLAVE W/BASS

AFRO-CUBAN 6

THE GROOVE (BEMBE/NANIGO)

ABOUT IT

Stemming from West African drumming, this Afro-Cuban pattern can be heard in traditional music, street drumming, drum circles, jazz, and popular music. In traditional Cuban drumming, these rhythms were played on different size conga drums (quinto, conga, tumbadora), shakers, and bells by multiple players using varying patterns. On the drum set, these different patterns can be recreated using the voices of the kit. In jazz and popular music, the *Afro-Cuban 6* can be incorporated into the shuffle, swing groove, or be played on its own. I use this groove frequently on gigs and it is a rhythm that every drummer should know.

LISTEN TO IT
- *Afro Blue* by Mango Santamaria
- *Incident at Neshabar* by Santana
- *Fridge* by Art Bernstein and Chuck D'Aloia

LEARN IT: BREAKDOWN

STEP 1: ONE HAND

Play just the cymbal pattern on the hi-hat, ride cymbal, or rim.
This played with the right, but it can also be played with the left (if you are a lefty).

STEP 2: TWO HANDS

On a drum pad or snare drum, play just the sticking pattern for both hands. Once you have this down, put it on the hi-hat and snare drum.

STEP 3: BASS & CYMBAL
Add the bass drum while playing just the cymbal pattern (right hand).

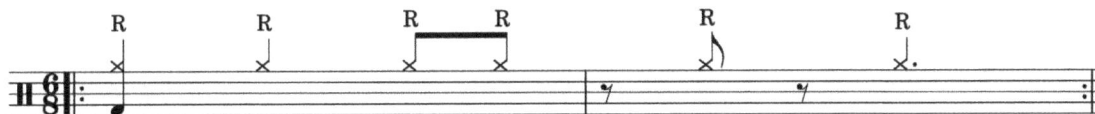

STEP 4: ALL TOGETHER
Put all the parts together. If needed, add just a few notes at a time until you can play the entire two bar pattern.

PRO TIP
When playing the *Afro-Cuban 6*, be sure to really dig into the accent o the snare drum on beat one of the second bar. This will provide the backbeat, which is the essence of popular music and allow the groove to fit nicely into different styles.

WATCH IT
Find my Afro-Cuban 6 video at:
https://www.youtube.com/watch?v=UArzRU4SDbo&t=44s

AFRO-CUBAN 6: RHYTHMIC VARIATIONS

BEMBE/NANIGO

DOUBLE PARADIDDLE W/BASS

2 AGAINST 3

ELEVATING THE GROOVE

BEMBE MEETS DOUBLE PARADIDDLE

OVER THE BAR

BOLERO

THE GROOVE

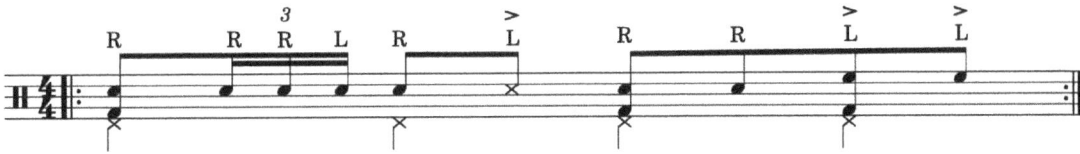

ABOUT IT

The Cuban bolero is a dance rhythm that dates back to the late 1800s. This groove has a fun little triplet at the beginning and accented eighth notes on beat four. Initially played on guitar to accompany singers, the groove mimics the guitarist's strumming patterns. The drum set version of the bolero is based on the rhythms played on a conga, which can be heard on tunes like Benny More's *Camarera del Amor*. When playing this rhythm, it is important to bring out beat one, up beat of two, and beat four, as this is how it is played on hand drums. This groove should be played with the snares off to replicate the hand drum sound.

LISTEN TO IT
- *Escondalo* by Mark Anthony
- *Camarera del Amor* by Benny More
- *Casi un Bolero* by Ricky Martin

LEARN IT: BREAKDOWN

STEP 1: HANDS ONLY

Learn the snare drum part, which should be played with the snares off. The basic sticking is R RRL R L R R L L. Note: The left hand on the upbeat of two is played as a cross stick.

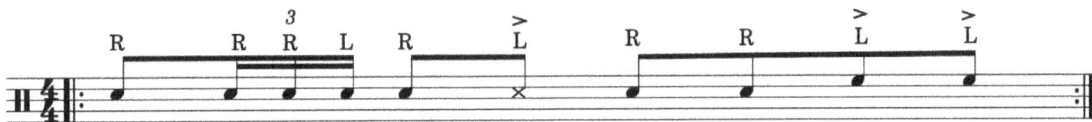

STEP 2: ADD BASS

Add the bass drum on one while playing the snare drum rhythm.

STEP 3: ADD HI-HAT (LEFT FOOT)

Play quarter notes on the hi-hat with your foot. Then, add the snare drum part.

STEP 4: ALL TOGETHER

Last, play the bass drum and hi-hat parts together. Once this is comfortable add the snare drum part.

PRO TIP

When playing the bolero, the snare drum part should be approached like it is a conga drum, which puts an emphasis on the clicks (simulating conga slaps) and accents on beat four (open tones on the conga).

WATCH IT

Find my Bolero video at: https://www.youtube.com/watch?v=Jt-mtB54UBc&t=22s

BOLERO: RHYTHMIC VARIATIONS

BASIC BOLERO

ALL SNARE

HI-HAT BOLERO

ELEVATING THE GROOVE

HI-HAT VARIATION

SNARE VARIATION W/HI-HAT

SONGO

THE GROOVE

ABOUT IT

Songo is a style of Cuban pop and jazz that blends Afro-Cuban and funk rhythms. While most Afro-Cuban music is traditionally played on timbales, congas, claves, and other instruments, the songo's origins are on the drum set. When playing with the group Lo Van Van the drummer Jose "Changuito" Luis Quintana created this rhythm on his drum set with no cymbals. Overtime, the style evolved to incorporate drum set and timbale hybrid; plus, the addition of a conga player. This groove uses a linear drum pattern, which means that each part is played one at a time.

LISTEN TO IT

- *Disco Azúcar* by Juan Formell y Los Van Van
- *Caribe Michel Camilo.*
- *Iya* by Irakere

LEARN IT: BREAKDOWN

STEP 1: ONE HAND

Play just the ride cymbal part with the right hand (reverse if you are a lefty). Note: This groove is in cut time.

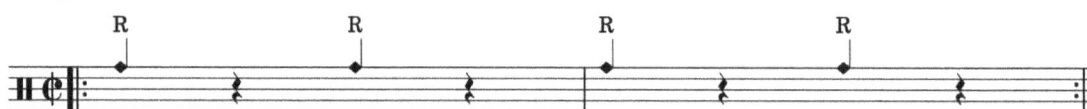

STEP 2: TWO HANDS

Now, play both hands. Pay special attention to the syncopated rhythms, as this will be important when adding the bass drum in the open spaces.

STEP 3: BASS & CYMBAL

Continue playing just the ride cymbal and add the bass drum. Notice that the bass drum is a syncopated ostinato, which is a repeated rhythmic pattern.

STEP 4: ALL TOGETHER

Last, slowly put all three parts together. Take your time with this step, as none of the parts are played at the same time. This is what makes it a linear pattern.

PRO TIP

The key to mastering this groove is independence, which will allow you to play freely over the bass and hi-hat pattern. To do this, I recommend starting with the variations in this book, then improvising over the ostinato bass drum and hi-hat pattern that never changes.

WATCH IT

Find my Songo video at:

https://www.youtube.com/watch?v=MhO6YOgUTKQ&t=57s

SONGO: RHYTHMIC VARIATIONS

2:3 CLAVE SONGO

CONGA STYLE

SYNCOPATED TOM

ELEVATING THE GROOVE

TRADITIONAL SONGO WITH HI-HAT

2:3 CLAVE WITH THREES

100

ABOUT THE AUTHOR

John Owens is a drummer, author, and educator with a single mission, which is to *build skillful, confident, and strong drummers*. John worked as a drummer in the US Army Band, street drummer in Washington DC, drummer for Disneyland, percussionist at Knott's Berry Farm, and toured/played with a vast number of jazz, rock, pop, country, and punk bands in the United States and Europe. In addition, John teaches college drumming and percussion, has written books about unique forms of drumming, such as *Street Drumming: The People History & Grooves*, and serves as a drum consultant for a number of schools, non-profit organizations, and ensembles. John Owens earned his Ph.D. in Music from Kent State University.

For more info about the author, books on drumming, and drum resources, go to:

www.tacticaldrumming.com

TACTICAL DRUMMING

www.ingramcontent.com/pod-product-compliance
Lightning Source LLC
Chambersburg PA
CBHW080608090426
42735CB00017B/3371